The Aesthetics of the Oppressed

'We must all do theatre – to find out who we are, and to discover who we could become.'

Augusto Boal – legendary Brazilian theatre director and creator of Theatre of the Oppressed – is back, with a stunning new collection of essays and stories.

Boal's vision of the transformative power of theatre reaches new heights with this latest polemic against globalisation and the sedative effects of Hollywood and television.

'To resist, it is not enough to say No – it is necessary to desire!'

The Aesthetics of the Oppressed describes the basis of a practical theatre project which enables individuals to reclaim themselves as subjects. Its central message is that we can discover Art by discovering our own creativity, and by discovering our creativity we discover ourselves.

In this latest despatch, Boal communicates his inspirational vision – articulating and expanding upon the practical and theoretical foundations of the work which over the last thirty years has become a vibrant international theatre movement.

Augusto Boal is a theatre director, dramatist, theorist, writer and teacher. He was a Member of Parliament for Rio de Janeiro from 1993 to 1996. He is the author of *The Theatre of the Oppressed*, *Games for Actors and Non-Actors*, *The Rainbow of Desire*, *Legislative Theatre* and *Hamlet and the Baker's Son: my life in theatre and politics*.

Adrian Jackson is Artistic Director of Cardboard Citizens. This is his fifth translated book by Augusto Boal. He has made and taught Theatre of the Oppressed practice widely in many countries; recent theatre work includes a co-production of *Pericles* with the Royal Shakespeare Company and a national tour of *Visible* by Sarah Woods.

D0165755

For information about the activities of Augusto Boal and the centres of Theatre of the Oppressed, please contact:

Centro do Teatro do Oprimido
Avenida Mem de Sá, 31
Arcos da Lapa – Centro
Rio de Janeiro – RJ – Brazil
Tel. (00 55 21) 2232 5826 / 2215 0503
Email: ctorio@ctorio.org.br

The Aesthetics of the Oppressed

Augusto Boal

Translated by Adrian Jackson

Routledge
Taylor & Francis Group

LONDON AND NEW YORK

First published 2006
by Routledge
2 Park Square, Milton Park, Abingdon, Oxon OX14 4RN

Simultaneously published in the USA and Canada
by Routledge
270 Madison Avenue, New York, NY 10016

*Routledge is an imprint of the Taylor & Francis Group,
an informa business*

© 2006 Augusto Boal
© 2006 Translation: Routledge

Typeset in Janson by Keystroke, Jacaranda Lodge, Wolverhampton

Printed and bound in Great Britain by The Cromwell Press,
Trowbridge, Wiltshire

British Library Cataloguing in Publication Data
A catalogue record for this book is available from the British Library

Library of Congress Cataloging in Publication Data
A catalog record for this book has been requested

ISBN10: 0–415–37176–7 (Hbk)
ISBN10: 0–415–37177–5 (Pbk)
ISBN10: 0–203–96983–9 (ebk)

ISBN13: 978–0–415–37176–6 (Hbk)
ISBN13: 978–0–415–37177–3 (Pbk)
ISBN13: 978–0–203–96983–0 (ebk)

Contents

CONTENTS

The dance teacher

When you live theatre, you live in emotion. After luminous Barcelona, illuminated Paris and snowy London, at the beginning of March 2002, I went to work in a hamlet of 10,000 souls, Hebden Bridge, in the middle of England.

In my time as a legislator, I had already done Theatre of the Oppressed with blind people in Rio de Janeiro, with deaf people in France, and with people with a variety of disabilities in other cities around the world. In Hebden Bridge I worked with deaf people, blind people, sufferers from cerebral palsy, Down's syndrome, multiple sclerosis and deep depression – all together within a single group; twenty people with different conditions and several 'carers', who are not nurses, but may perform that function at times and much more besides.

Why had they come from afar to work with me? I had met Susan Quick in a workshop I led in Derry, in Northern Ireland, ten years back. She liked my way of doing theatre so much that she went on to teach it in various war-torn African countries, where she worked for seven years. Returning to reside in her homeland, after having faced so many dangers abroad, what with bombs and grenades, she was driving her car peacefully back from an excursion, coming along a hillside in darkest winter when fog and night had turned to ice, only to spin off the road thirty metres from her door, and come careering off a ridge. She was left partly paralysed.

This did not stop her from doing theatre and she went on to lead workshops for others like herself, who had some kind of physical or mental disability. I hardly need to say that my workshop with her group was one of the most difficult pieces of work of my life; never had my attention, or my care for the group, been more concentrated on each and every one of my pupils.

Of them, two seemed to me to demand particularly tender handling: Sig, a very slender woman less than forty years of age and less than forty kilos body weight, needed her carer to amplify her voice, so weak was her body, so enfeebled her lungs; seated in a wheelchair, twice a session she flopped down onto a mattress to rest. She had lost her parents in Johannesburg, when her house was blown up, during the *apartheid* era. Sig lived with relatives, and an assistant paid by the state.

Alan journeyed for two hours on the train, twice a day, from Liverpool and back; a sufferer from cerebral palsy, he was unable to coordinate his arms and legs, or to speak words or even syllables – thanks to the miracle of electronics, he communicated with us by means of a computer, *Dynavox*, which offered a range of generic signs which in turn led to more specific signs; with difficulty Alan could strike the relevant keys. Having formed the phrase, he would hit the 'ENTER' key and the computer would pronounce the script in a metallic voice. When the machine did not suffice, his assistant interpreted his facial expressions, and the look in his eyes.

Sig and Alan participated in the short pieces which laid bare their oppressions and, intrepidly took to the stage whenever they wanted to theatricalise their opinions and their desires – each in their own rhythm – and we always respect the rhythm of each individual.

On the last day, during the goodbyes, I asked Alan what he did in his normal life, when he was not spending all this time on the train. He answered that he liked music and was a teacher. By this time, Alan knew how to read my face, and he read my amazement: a teacher of what?

'I am a dance teacher!'

Even greater amazement! His assistant came to my aid and translated his thoughts: before the onset of his illness, Alan was a dance teacher and, like Susan, he had dedicated himself after his own illness to others who suffered the same condition. He would explain to his pupils the origin and characteristics of the tango, the rumba, the bolero and the samba. Then they would listen to CDs and, each in his own way would dance – moving arms, face, eyes even – re-inventing the dance.

What is dance if not the body passionately marrying itself to the rhythm? If you are born Nureyev you can perform acrobatic leaps; if you are less elastic, you dance in your wheelchair. It's all dance! As long as we are alive, we are all dancers, even the fat woman who lives next door and her stubby-legged husband!

Still moved, I took my leave of Sig, who told me she had learnt a great deal in the workshop, which, to my judgement, had been excessively body-oriented for her circumstances. I asked her if she had got anything out of it. Happy to answer, through her assistant, she thanked me;

'Sure – I got a lot out of it: every day, at least twice a day, I smiled.'

She smiled . . . and I almost wept.

The smile, more than laughter or tears, is the sweetest way of giving meaning to our lives.

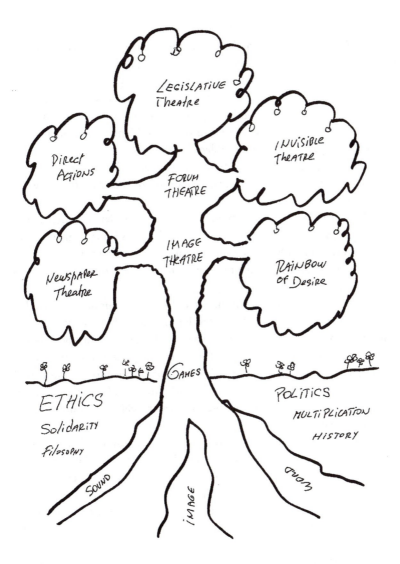

'The Tree of the Theatre of the Oppressed' by Augusto Boal

The tree of the theatre of the oppressed

Since 1970, when I systematised the Techniques of *Newspaper Theatre*, the *Theatre of the Oppressed* method has not stopped growing, in Brazil and in the five continents, always adding new Techniques which respond to new necessities, and never abandoning any of the old ones.

The enormous diversity of Techniques and of their possible applications – in social and political struggle, in psychotherapy, in pedagogy, in town as in country, in the treatment of immediate problems in one area of the city or in the great economic problems of the whole country – has never deflected them, not by one millimetre even, from their original informing proposition, which is the unwavering support of the theatre in the struggles of the oppressed.

Rather than being made up of a number of isolated, independent Techniques, a strict relationship between all the parts is maintained within this diversity, and all have the same origin in the fertile ground of Ethics and Politics, of History and Philosophy, from which our tree draws its nutrient sap.

Extending beyond the usual frontiers of the theatre, our new project, *The Aesthetics of the Oppressed*, seeks to develop, in those that practise it, their capacity to perceive the world by means of all the arts and not only the theatre, centring this process on *The Word* (all participants must write poems and narratives); *The Sound* (the invention of new instruments and of new sounds); and *The Image* (painting, sculpture and photography). Each leaf of this tree forms an indissoluble part of it, reaching right down to the roots and the earth.

The fruits which fall to the ground serve to reproduce themselves by *Multiplication*. The synergy created by the Theatre of the Oppressed increases its transformatory power in ratio to the extent that it expands and succeeds in interlinking different groups of oppressed people; these need to know not only their own oppressions, but also oppressions which are foreign to them. *Solidarity* with our fellows is an essential part of the Theatre of the Oppressed.

On the trunk of the tree grow, first, the *Games*, because they bring together two essential characteristics of life in society; they have rules, as does society, which are necessary in order for the *Games* to be enacted; but they also require creative freedom, so that the *Game*, or life, is not transformed into servile obedience. Without rules, there is no game, without freedom, there is no life.

Apart from this essential metaphoric characteristic, *Games* help enable the de-mechanisation of the body and the mind alienated by the repetitive tasks of the day-to-day, particularly those related to work and to the economic, environmental and social conditions of those who take part in them.

The body, in work as in play, as well as producing stimuli, responds to those it receives, creating, in itself, a *muscular mask* as strong as the mask of *social behaviour* – both of which act directly on the thought and emotions which thus become stratified. *Games* facilitate and oblige this de-mechanisation, being, as they are, sensory dialogues where, within the necessary discipline, they demand the creativity which is their essence.

The word is the greatest invention of the human being, and yet it brings with it the obliteration of the senses, the atrophy of other forms of perception.

Art is the search for truths by means of our sensory equipment. In *Image Theatre*, we dispense with the use of the word – which, however, we revere! – so that we can develop other forms of perception. We use the body, physiognomies, objects, distances and colours, which oblige us to enlarge our *signalétique* vision – where signifiers and signifieds are indissociable, like the smile of joy on our face, or the tears of sadness and lamentation – rather than only using the *symbolic* language of words dissociated from concrete, sensible realities, to which they refer only by means of sound or mark on paper.

Newspaper Theatre – ten techniques involving the transformation of journalistic texts into theatrical scenes – consists of the combination of Images and Words to reveal in the former, meanings which are hidden in the latter. It shows, for example, that in their own way newspapers use techniques of fiction, just as literature does: layout, column size, the placing of each piece of news within the pages of the paper, etc.

Newspaper Theatre serves to demystify the pretended impartiality of the media. If papers, magazines, radio and TV stations are economically dependent on their advertisements, they will never allow genuine information or news items which reveal their origin or what interests they serve or question the veracity of their publisher – the media will always be used to please those that sustain them: they will always be the voice of their master!

The same analytical process occurs with the Introspective Techniques of the *Rainbow of Desires* which, using words and, especially, images, enables the theatricalisation of introjected oppressions. In these Techniques – which revolve on each of us as individuals, whilst always seeking resonances of the group – even in these Techniques, which are part of the Tree of Theatre of the Oppressed (TO), the objective is to show that these internalised oppressions have their origin in, and retain an intimate relation with, our social life. One of the main techniques, *The Cop in the Head*, shows that, if an internal oppression exists, it is because it comes from some barracks or other, exterior to the subjectivity of the subject.

Forum Theatre: perhaps the most democratic form of the Theatre of the Oppressed and certainly the best known and most practised throughout the world, uses or can use all the resources of all known theatrical forms. Those we call *Spect-actors* are invited to come on stage and reveal by means of theatre – rather than by just using words – the thoughts, desires and strategies that can suggest, to the group to which they belong, a palette of possible alternatives of their own invention. This theatre should be a rehearsal for action in real life, rather than an end in itself.

The show is the beginning of a necessary social transformation and not a moment of equilibrium and repose. *The end is the beginning!*

The *Theatre of the Oppressed*, in all its forms, is always seeking the trans-formation of society in the direction of the liberation of the oppressed. It is both action in itself, and a preparation for future actions. As we all know, it is not enough to interpret reality: it is necessary to transform it!

These transformations can be sought also in actions rehearsed and realised theatrically, but as theatre in an un-revealed form, to a chance audience, not conscious of their condition of spectator. An interpenetration of fiction into reality and of reality into fiction: all those present can intervene at any moment in the search for solutions for the problems being treated. The *Invisible* show can be presented in any location where its drama could really occur or has already occurred (in the street or the square, in the supermarket or the fair, in the queue for the bus or the cinema . . .). Actors and audience meet on the same level of dialogue and power. There is no antagonistic relationship between the auditorium and stage, rather the two are superposed.

This is *Invisible Theatre*.

Direct Actions (in the context of the Theatre of the Oppressed) involve the theatricalisation of protest demonstrations, peasants' marches, secular processions, parades, meetings of workers or other organised groups, street commissions, etc., using all available theatrical elements, such as masks, songs, dances, choreography, etc.

Finally, even knowing that in Brazil, at least – but I believe everywhere – laws do not often come from simple suggestions and they do not always 'take root', as they say, it is better to have them on our side than against us. *Legislative Theatre* is a set of processes which mixes *Forum Theatre* and the conventional rituals of a parliamentary chamber or assembly, with the objective of arriving at the formulation of coherent and viable bills of law. From this starting point, we then have to follow the normal route for their presentation in legislating chambers and put pressure on the legislators to approve them.

By this method, CTO Rio has already achieved the passing of fifteen municipal and two state laws.

The objective of the whole tree is to bring forth fruits, seeds and flowers: this is our desired goal, in order that the Theatre of the Oppressed may seek not only to understand reality, but to transform it to our liking.

We, the oppressed.

The aesthetics of
the oppressed

A THEORETICAL FOUNDATION

1 ANALOGICAL AND COMPLEMENTARY SETS

Nature never produces two identical creations: neither two grains of sand nor two hairs on my chin, not even twins born from a single egg, finger-prints or drops of rain, birds of the forest or its branches and leaves, or the veins of each leaf . . . nothing is absolutely identical to anything else. All inanimate things and all living beings are always unique and unrepeatable, even if cloned.

For any self-moving creature, whether human or animal, possessed of a minimum of psychic life, it would be impossible to live within this infinite diversity unless it could organise and simplify its perception of the world.

We would become paralysed if we had to see and be conscious of every-thing that we looked upon; if we had to listen to and be conscious of all that we heard; if we had to feel and be conscious of all that we touched, smelt and tasted – such would be the torrential and catastrophic accumulation of received information. Nature is vertiginous, but we cannot endure this vertigo on a day-to-day basis.

Happily, Nature allows the creation of simple semblances for complex realities, by means of the construction of *Analogical Sets* and *Complementary Sets*. Though simplifications exclude complexities, there is no other way, and we are forced to perform the psychic process of the formation of *Sets* in order to be able to live in this world and steer a course through it.

When a baby opens its eyes for the first time, it looks at everything its eyes alight on, and, looking at everything, sees nothing, only the colour grey. Little by little, as its optic nerve begins to be stimulated by light and shade, it organises its visual perception, distinguishing straight lines and curves, depths and colours.

The moment it ceases to *look* at everything at the same time, is the moment it really begins to see – and what it sees is *Sets*.

No fish is absolutely the same as another fish, but fish are alike; thus we have the shoal. No rose is the same as another rose, but, red, white or yellow, they all resemble each other – and so we have rose gardens. No colour is so homogenous in every extension of the object coloured that it is impossible to abstract different tones – differences which, when observed through a microscope, are quite clear and distinct.

An astronaut tells us the earth is blue; we say that the night is black, the blood in our veins red, and the rainy sky grey . . . We know that this is not so: no single millimetre is the same as another.

CTO-Rio Community Group: Arte Vida
Forum Theatre Play: A Princesa e o Plebeu (The Princess and the Plebian)
Subject: Discrimination against underpriveleged youth living in *favelas*
Directed by: Flávio Sanctum
Photographer: Carola Pagani (AFAB)
FESTEL (Legislative Theatre Festival 2005 – Rio de Janeiro, Brazil)

By the use of analogy, we can perceive and form *Analogical Sets*, which are homogenous, which consist of things which are similar, but not the same – i.e. *Unicities*[1] within a greater whole – like the *corps de ballet*, the chorus of an opera, a battalion of soldiers or the flour of a single sack.

We can also perceive heterogeneous sets, made up of complementary elements. No two rivers run exactly the same course, but water runs in all rivers – whether in the abundant Amazon or the smallest brook in the mountain. Their banks may be different, but all oppress the waters which run between them. Likewise the stones on the river beds are not the same in weight or form, but similar, even when made of different organic or mineral material.

We can perceive the forest as a *Set* of similar trees, knowing full well they are not all the same;[2] or the herd as a *Set* of animals of the same species, even though each member of this herd will have its own particular nature, its own particular snout, its own particular hunger. We can see the crowd as a *Set* of human beings – though none of them will be the same as any one of us.

Even the same individual, or the same thing, is a heterogeneous *Set*, made up of *Complementary* elements: we have a head, a neck, a trunk and limbs, arteries and veins, hair and skin; a stone has many colours, even when it is grey, and rich variations of form in its surface, even when designated 'round'.

Thus, by simplifying our perception of Nature, we can live without shocks: *Unicities* can be systematised into *Analogical Sets* of similar beings and things, or *Complementary Sets* of dissimilar things and beings. Lost in this simplification is the richness of differences and unique identities, which is forever inaccessible.

This simplification, which is the work of our imagination and not of multifarious Nature, functions like an armour which allows us access only to the appearances of the real[3] and, on these appearances, we can predicate.

So that we humans can communicate between ourselves, these sets must be named: we give the name 'mountain' to all protuberances from the earth that kiss the sky, knowing full well that no mountain is the same as any other mountain, no cloud the same as any other cloud, no dream the same as mine. We name as *sea* all waved agglomerations, whether of water, sunflowers, people . . . – the *sea* of the drunken people on New Year's Eve, a *sea* of flowers in the wind, the watery *sea* of raging waves.

Naming signifies the effort to immobilise. The name is the fixing, in time and space, of that which is fluid, that which actually cannot stop or be stopped in time or space.

All is in transit, even I, when they name me Augusto Boal. Which Augusto Boal? Am I the one I was before writing this last line or the person who has not yet written the next?

I am one of Cratilus's[4] rivers: in me, run waters that did not run before, and other waters will run after, and never will these waters flow back to the river behind them – always flowing down to hide in the sea.

No-one can see me twice as I am, in each fleeting instant of my life, as all instants are fleeting . . . as is life. I will never be the same, each second that steals away from me. And similarly, those who see me now will never be the same as themselves in any two successive seconds of the trajectory of their paths through life.

I *am* not; I am *being*. As a traveller, I am passing from one state to another. I am not; I came and I go. I hesitate: where to? I invent my paths, if I can, or I go forwards, if obliged!

2 WORDS AS MEANS OF TRANSPORT

Words designate *Sets*, but ignore *Unicities*. Blacks and whites, men and women, proletarian and peasant are imagined as *Sets*, but do not exist as concretion. They *are*, but they do not *exist*. What exists, corporeally, is *this* particular black person and *that* particular white person, *this* woman and *that* man, *this* peasant and *that* worker – and even then, all of these are in transit, in the state of becoming, of coming to be and ceasing to be. None of them is the same as it was, from one moment to the next, in this permanent state of becoming.

Living sets, given the strength that unites them, can react as if they were unicities: a military unit or a football team, a united family or a union on strike. A *Set* is always more than the sum of its units – it is a synergy.

For the process of exchange and dialogue to be possible among humans, words – *above all, names* – are indispensable, and yet they are *polysemic signifiers* that, when perceived by their receiver, lose a large part of the meanings which motivated their sender and acquire new meanings according to each receiver.

When pronounced by the sender, the words are signifiers rich with significations of the experiences of this sender, of his memories, desires and imagination; in transit, these signifiers change their significations, like a lorry changing cargo, from one city to the next. On arrival at the receiver, the words are loaded with the experiences of the latter and not the former.[5] Even if it arrives at its destination with its cargo untouched, the receiver has his own apparatus of translation-reception, which translate and betray the message received. As the Italians say, *Traduttore, traditore* – translator, traitor.

Words are a means of transport, like buses and lorries. In the same way as buses transport people and lorries cargo, words transport our ideas, desires and emotions. With the same word we can say exactly the opposite of what the dictionary states – in writing the phrase, by means of syntax, and in speaking the phrase, by means of the language of the voice – i.e the timbre, the tone, the volume, the pauses, etc.[6]

The first thing that a means of transport transports is itself: we can appreciate the beauty of a jet plane or of an old steam train, or an unusual word; but, to better understand them, we need to understand what they are carrying and who is sending them to us.

The word is a totality that is a Nothing. It is a mark we scratch in the sand; a sound we sculpt in the air, like demented sculptors – a sign borne away by the waves of the sea, a sound dissolving in the breeze.

Sand we feel in our hand, wind strokes our face. So what about words? Where are they? Nowhere, since they don't exist; they merely are.

Words are nowhere and everywhere. Words are the emptiness which fills the emptiness that exists between one human being and another.

Scratching the sand or cleaving the air, in this emptiness we deposit our lives, our desires, our fears, our courage, our feelings and our emotions – behold the word. We fill this nothing with everything that we are; we are the words that we speak and the words are us, transformed into sounds and marks.

For words to acquire a meaning more precise and less permissive, they need to be dressed: in Greek tragedy, with mask, *cothornus*[7] and cloak; in the temple, with its liturgy; in the army, with hierarchical discipline; in the cinema, with lighting, camera angles and lenses. In daily life, with our clothes, our cultural signs, the timbres and rhythms of our speech, our physiognomy.

For us to be able to apprehend the Singular, the One, rather than merely the Sets to which it belongs, the intervention of some other form of mediation becomes necessary, to avoid the imprecision of our giving the same name, 'cow', to each member of the herd of cattle – since this livestock is made up of unrepeatable bovine unicities, not mere butchers' mass. Each cow has its own personality: it is a Singular being – it is the One called Mimosa, Star, Mimi, or whatever. The herd is a synergy.

Words are the work and the instruments of reason: we have to transcend them and look for forms of communication which are not just rational, but also sensory – aesthetic communications. This aesthetic transcendence of reason is the reason for theatre and for all the arts. We cannot divorce reason and feeling, idea and form. They are a constant couple, even when at loggerheads, even when they come to blows.[8]

3 THE EVIL THAT WORDS DO

Words are so powerful that, when we hear or speak them, we sometimes override our own senses – through which, without the intervention of words, we would perceive the signals of the world more clearly. Our comprehension of words is slow because they need to be decoded, in contrast to feelings and sensations, which are immediately perceptible – this is the main difference between languages which are symbolic and languages which are what the French call *signalétique*,[9] between symbols and signs.

If I hear a word, whatever it is, I need some time to comprehend its meaning and the intentions of my interlocutor. But if I put my finger on an uninsulated wire, the electric shock I get does not require any special translation. I scream!

Animals, who do not talk or exchange ideas amongst themselves, even when necessary – as for instance, Brecht's cows on the way to the slaughterhouse – depend exclusively on their senses for their comprehension of the world. Or a bull facing the matador's sword in a crowded bullring: it would prefer to engage in dialogue and come to an agreement with the bullfighter, rather than just fight – unfortunately, the bull lacks words. What a pity for it.

The point in prehistoric times at which human beings started to babble the first words of the proto-proto universal language, was the point at which the slow degradation of their senses began.

The supposed existence of this primitive universal language, as mentioned in the Bible, was scientifically defended by the North American linguists Joseph Greenberg and Merritt Ruhlen, from 1980 onwards.

According to them, all the languages spoken in the world, now and in the past, can be systematised and reunited in different families (such as, for instance, the family which reunites the Romance, Slavic and Germanic languages). These families are, hypothetically, descendants of a single Proto-Language, the so-called Indo-European language which perhaps was spoken by a nomadic people three to six thousand years before us. Joining this and other Proto-Languages leads to the formation of a huge genealogical tree with a common trunk: the proto-proto-language, the first universal language. This theory has its logic, even for a person who does not believe in Adam and Eve.

A tragic example of human senses weakened by the rise of speech – and the dislocation of our attention from signs and signals to symbols – happened on 26 December 2004, when a powerful tsunami devastated a number of cities in Asia and Africa, killing more than 300,000 people. However, in the National Park in Sri Lanka none of the wild animals died, in spite of the terrible flooding caused by the powerful 13 metre-high waves. Elephants and jackals, birds and rodents, even the clumsy crocodiles, all managed to escape. All fled in time, moving to more elevated areas when they noticed the first seismic vibrations and the first distant rumblings of the ocean floor as it opened.

Only domestic animals died . . . already contaminated by the words they heard, even without understanding them.

This tragedy does not diminish the supreme value of the Word as a refined means of communication, but it reveals a displacement of pure perception – signs displaced by symbols – which brings with it a sad downside, due to the fact that we have to translate symbols, and this takes time.

While the sea rose around them, Asians and Africans awaited symbolic warnings – words – by telephone or megaphone, TV, radio or telegram, not paying attention to the seismic signals that their bodies were registering, but which did not reach their consciousnesses – sensations which were not transformed into messages, information that was not transformed into knowledge.

4 FROM AESTHETIC PROCESS TO ARTISTIC PRODUCT

The Artist is, like any of us, a person who is capable of seeing *Sets* in which analogies and complementarities unify things which are not the same – for this reason, he or she can live in society. However, not confining themselves to the conjunctive vision which we use to perceive reality, by means of *Analogical* or *Complementary Sets*, or by the words we use to communicate – since words are *symbols* which designate *Sets* – Artists move forward, penetrating the real and revealing, both in their aesthetic way of doing things (research, work, trial and error) and in their artistic product (the finished work of art)[10] perceptions and unique aspects of that armour-plated reality. The artist perceives and reveals unicities hidden by the simplification of the language which names them and the senses which group them without perceiving them.

The Artist penetrates the unicity of the being, as if searching for his or her complement, or searching for him – or herself – for his or her Identity in Alterity. The Singular seeks the Singular, the One seeking Oneself in the Other.[11]

This dynamic perception never comes to a halt, but rather increases or diminishes in intensity, always fluid both for the artist in relation to her

CTO-Rio Community Group: **Marias do Brasil**
Forum Theatre Play: **Eu também sou Mulher (I Too Am A Woman)**
Subject: **Working rights of housemaids**
Directed by: **Claudete Felix and Olivar Bendelak**
Photographer: **Gustavo Bezerra**
Legislative Theatre Activity: **Presentation inside the Brazilian Federal Parliament on 25 November 2004 – Brasília, Brazil**

work and the lover in relation to the loved one. Loves are overcome and lost, at the whim of life . . . and depending on the dominion we can achieve over life. Like art, which is always in flux.

Though only some people are given the title of Artist, the truth is that each and every human being is, *substantively*, an artist. We all possess, to some degree or other, the capacity to penetrate unicities, whether by making art or making love. We are all capable of encounter with the Singular.

It is important to note the distinction which I make here between the *making*, that is, the Aesthetic Process, and the *thing once it is already finished*, or the Artistic Product. Process and Product – for the latter to exist, the former is necessary; though the Aesthetic Process does not necessarily have to result in an Artistic Product – it can be inconclusive. This will, however, be where we aim.

For the Aesthetics of the Oppressed, the most important thing is the Aesthetic Process which develops the perceptions of the person who practises it, though it may be very desirable that it culminates in an Artistic Product – the finished work of art – for its amplificatory social power. The goal of fruition as work of Art is stimulating – it functions like a search for the dream, for utopia. When the process does culminate in this state, its authors receive the benefits of the recognition of others, which encourages them to make further efforts.

The Aesthetic Process allows the subjects to exercise themselves in activities which are usually denied them, thus expanding their expressive and perceptive possibilities.

Each cerebral stimulus relating to one area of human activity stimulates adjacent or related areas in the brain: the brain is an ecosystem and not a computer's hard disk. It is elastic and plastic. For this reason, the Aesthetic Process is useful in itself, and becomes more useful when it arrives at the production of an Artistic Product which can be shared with other persons.

The Artistic Product – the work of art – must be capable of awakening, even in those who did not participate in the Aesthetic Process by which it came into being, the same ideas, emotions and thoughts that led the artist to its creation.

We should be clear about the fact that the Aesthetic Process is not the Work of Art. Its importance and its value reside in its stimulation and development of perceptive and creative capacities which may be atrophied in the subject – in developing the capacity, however small it may be, that every subject has for metaphorising reality.

We are all artists, but few of us exercise our aesthetic capacities.

5 LOVE AND ART

Art is love. The loved one is the Only Being, discovered by the lover and by her alone. When we love, we see and feel the loved one as irreplaceable and irreproducible. When we love, we penetrate the unicity of the loved one who, in turn, is a complex one-person universe, in constant movement. Precisely because this movement is constant, love is not! Which is why, on meeting again his former love, now forgotten, Proust's Swann can say: 'She is not even my type . . .'. She *is not* now, but, at the time that they pursued each other, and in the journey they travelled together, she *was*!

Love, which is an aesthetic experience, though founded in reality, is a work of the imagination: in loving, we love not only the person who concretely exists, but the projections we make on her – projections which are product and part of ourselves. Our imagination projects onto our beloved, vices and virtues which she does not have, but which exist in our desire or our fear. That explains why many people are afraid to be loved: they feel that what is being loved is a projection made on them which tends to immobilise them and adapt them to that projection. In his film *L'Avventura*, Michelangelo Antonioni shows a man who runs away every time he feels that a woman is falling in love with him. This is unbearable to him: she is loving the fixed image she has made of him, a man in constant transformation. He ends up on a couch with a prostitute, but takes care to pay her before he leaves: he ceases to be himself and becomes a 'client'.

Loving is Art, and Art is Love. These two processes – loving, and perceiving aesthetically the unicity of the Other, whether living Being or Thing – are absolutely identical. More, even, they are the same thing.[12]

In Love as in Art, the two being identical, our perception of the Other or the Thing, does not become set or immobilised. Love is the flow of alternating current – as electricity can be and as the seas are but without any guarantee of constant or predictable rhythms, never the same, always at the whim of constant variation.

Eternal loves do exist – especially the kind which end early in bloody tragedy – and so do perennial works of art, but neither the person loved, nor the work admired, are loved or admired with a constant intensity, or for the same reasons at any given moment in time.

In love and in art, the only constant is inconstancy.

Contrary to what they say, Love is not a meeting: it is a pursuit!

One person who is always changing pursues another person who is never the same as him- or herself.

Love offers no guarantee of stability. Just as we must cultivate Art with love, the cultivation of Love is an art.

6 ART AND KNOWLEDGE

To gain access to these ultimate and unique realities, we have artists, whose aesthetic activities – that is, activities related to the senses – capture unicities and allow us to know true reality, which is always unique.[13] In Art, as *Aesthetic Process*, and in the Work of Art, as finished article, as *Artistic Product*, the human being enters into contact with the real – as in passionate orgasm or in delirium.

In this sense, Art is a special form of knowledge – subjective, sensory, not scientific. It is not better than other forms of knowledge, but it is unique. The artist, in the exercise of her Art, voyages beyond the appearances of the real and penetrates unicities hidden by *Sets*;[14] in the *Work of Art*, she synthesises her voyage with the essence of the real and creates a new *Set* – the Work – which reveals the Singular discovered in this dive to the depths; and this Singular, by analogy, remits us to ourselves where some analogical or complementary singularities also exist which allow us to enjoy the Work.

When I hear the stern opening chords of Beethoven's Fifth, or the tremulous aria *Voi que sapete*, sung by Cherubino in Mozart's *Marriage of Figaro*, or Verdi's sad *La Traviata*, in each case these are unique harmonies that I am hearing, amidst the anarchic infinity of noises and sounds which explode in my way. Some unique thing, hidden in some unique place within me, awakens and vibrates, and makes me vibrate, like a human being – that is Art.

We vibrate as artists hearing unique harmonies, structured in a unique manner. Through this unicity, by analogy, a new imaginary *Set* is arrived at, which we call *audience*, made up of those people who feel some identity – not rational, but rationalisable – with such chords, or with Hamlet or Lear, or the Mona Lisa smile, Aleijadinho's saints,[15] or the Venus de Milo (which, of necessity, cannot have the arms she once had: if she had them, she would be something other than she is – the absence of her arms reveals the presence of time, which we also enjoy).

The *I* is transformed into an *us* – extraordinary leap. In this *us* and in each *I*, we *discover the discovery* that the artist made. When we are able to speak of *us*, we become the sum of all our relations and something more, as in any synergy.

Metaphorically, I am sounds and forms, rhythms and colours, I am Wagner and Velazquez. Even if I have never sung like the Valkyries and never painted drunks or little girls.

Art rediscovers and reinvents reality from a singular perspective: that of the artist, who is unique, as is his relationship with the real, and his way of seeing and feeling – from which is born the Work of Art, capable of recreating, in each of us, the same path of the artist. This reality, as seen by the artist, can only be observed starting from his Work, which is also unique.[16]

The scientist does the same, but from an anonymous perspective which belongs to all and does not depend on the individuality of the solitary scientist. Pythagoras's Theorem reveals that, in a right-angled triangle, the square of the hypotenuse is always equal to the sum of the squares on the two shorter sides, and this will be the case whatever the country, whatever the time of day or night, in summer as in winter, whoever the drawer of the triangle, whatever the colour of his hair. Newton swore that all matter attracts all other matter with a force proportional to the product of their masses and inversely proportional to the square of the distance between them – and this is true, in earth as in heaven, come rain or shine. It does not matter that, much later, Einstein introduced the idea that space curves when close to the mass of any matter – for those of us who live with our feet on the ground, the best advice I can give is 'Keep away from apple trees . . .'.

Science is an art, but art is not science. Art doesn't give an account of all of actual reality, but it is actually a reality.

7 AESTHETICS AND NEURONS

The Aesthetics of the Oppressed is based on the scientific fact that in any individual when the neurons of sensory perception – the cells of the nervous system – are activated, these neurons do not get filled up, like the bytes in a computer, storing aesthetic information. They neither empty nor fill – *knowledge does not take up space*, as common sense tells us! In contrast to solitary bytes, when stimulated, neurons form circuits which become ever more capable of receiving and transmitting more and more simultaneous messages – sensory or motor, abstract or emotional – enriching their functionality and activating neighbouring neurons so that they too go into action, creating ever greater networks of linked circuits which make us *remember* other circuits, establishing *relations between circuits* which maintain some semblance or affinity between themselves, which enables us to *create, invent, imagine.*

Imagination is memory transformed by desire.

The neurons are already starting to be produced in the foetus, in an accelerated manner, by the third week of uterine life. They are all similar, with no specialisation. Depending on where they are to be finally installed, they are specialised in the function that they will need there: they are plastic. If they go to the auditory nerve, they specialise in transmitting sounds to the cerebral cortex; if to the optic nerve, images; and so on.

CTO-Rio Community Group: **Panela de Opressão**
Forum Theatre Play: **Acorda! O Sonho Acabou (Wake up! The Dream is Over)**
Subject: **Sex education and teenage pregnancy**
Directed by: **Bárbara Santos**
Photographer: **Carola Pagani (AFAB)**
FESTEL (Legislative Theatre Festival 2005 – Rio de Janeiro, Brazil)

The messages received by the cortex – sounds, images, smells, tastes, cutaneous sensations, ideas, physiognomies – transformed into neuron circuits, relate with other circuits already existing in deeper and more fixed strata of the brain, and can be carried back to the cortex, where they will engage in *dialogue* with the new messages, a dialogue from which will emerge the subject's decisions.

All these modified circuits will return to the sub-cortical strata where they will influence the reception of new messages with which they retain some relationship. The primary sounds will influence the reception of new sounds; the primary images, new images; the old words will be confronted with new words; old concepts with new concepts; primary values with new values.

None of these *primary*, archaic elements are immutable. They can be modified, substituted or eradicated because they are not definitive – nothing in the human being is definitive! But they have influence.

8 THE INVASION OF OUR BRAINS

If the brain of a television viewer is filled with Hollywood-inspired films, void of ideas and full of brute force (which is their only form of dialogue), it stands to reason that these shots, bombs, explosions, punches and machine-gun volleys are going to influence this hapless viewer's future perception of the world. They are going to influence his decisions.

It is not the violence *per se* which causes damage to the viewer, but the lack of rationale for this physical activity. When dealing with Rambo and other 'super-heroes' of this sub-species, Empathy[17] plays a very dangerous role. *Empatheia*, in Greek, means the vicarious experience of feelings and thoughts of others – characters in the performing arts, or a real person in daily life. This is especially potent when imposed by the Protagonist in Tragedy on passive spectators.

When rational foundations of physical acts are not there, *Empathy* turns into a relationship of pure irrational animality. Continuous intimacy with brutality tends to form brutes. When a person lives in the wild in the company of savage predators, without the human presence, how will that person be humanised? Children abandoned in the jungle, who have been brought up by wild animals, never learn to smile. Violence in itself is neither good nor bad. Shakespeare is full of such things as the amputation of hands and the piercing of eyes. Violence is bad when unaccompanied by reason, when reduced to blows and punches, or supported only by simplistic, standard pre-conceived ideas. But it can be didactic when rationalised and when its causes and its Ethos are laid bare.

This type of cinematography owes its mediocrity not to the lack of its authors' creativity, but to the deliberate intention, by means of mechanical repetition, to block the intellectual development of its passive audiences, and stunt their capacity to create and to think in metaphor.

Stanley Kubrick's marvellous *Full Metal Jacket* shows with aesthetic perfection the ultra-military process by which peremptory orders to obey and to kill are implanted in the brains of army recruits. What this talented director demonstrates in this military example is the same process as occurs on TV for civilians, far from civilised as it is.

We are alarmed at the invasion of the Amazon rainforest by grasping foreign powers and home-grown landowners, who promote burning and clearance. Absolutely right, we should be alarmed about this! But yet more dangerous is the invasion of commercial Hollywood-style cinematography which already dominates and steers the lives of the greater part of our somnambulist tele-viewers.

We are not only talking of the hysterical nature of TV, but also hysterical music: even countries like Brazil – where every region creates dozens of fascinating rhythms – even these are invaded by mass-produced music invented and distributed by multinational companies.

In the same way as a US sociologist[18] sought to decree the end of History, the phonographic industry now wants to decree the end of Music. This tragic end has already been invented, ten years ago in Berlin: *techno*, a rhythm similar to a deformed and poor version of the pile-driver or the jack-hammer, except that these two pieces of building industry-related machinery are more musical, more delicate, and more sensitive than the *techno* monotone which, amongst other health hazards, interferes with pace-makers used by heart patients and has already caused several deaths in outdoor shows on the streets of Berlin.

Over and above film and music, the rest of the media robs political and economic facts of their importance, dedicating itself to the superfluous and the insignificant. Besides the end of History, the end of Music, the end of the Visual Arts, the end of Theatre and Cinema, and the end of Social Movements, the communication media want to decree the end of Thought.

For this design to be achieved it is necessary to empty words, to render them innocuous and, for this reason, the first step consists of purloining words like *Liberty* and *Democracy*, giving them meanings exactly opposite to the ones we know. Invoking Liberty and Democracy, one country invades other countries, tortures and kills its citizens, calls those who resist 'insurgents', stating that it is doing this to re-establish order. What kind of order? Order imposed by force.

This undue appropriation of signifieds and signifiers, this purposeful emptying of all the contents of the Word – which, being able to mean anything, ends up meaning nothing – has as its objective the destruction of the capacity of the citizen to make and use metaphor, the destruction of the capacity for any kind of reasoning through words or images.

The poisoning of words seeks to disorganise language and impede the formulation of coherent thought. We no longer know what we are saying when we speak. Language, spoken and written, becomes mysterious and inaccessible – it becomes an obstacle to communication, exactly the opposite of the purpose for which it was created.

It is not catastrophist exaggeration to say that we are mired in the Great World War of Dis-communication, an insidious and surreptitious, omnipotent and omniscient fifth column. The clear objective of this new modality of war is mastery, not of geographic territories, but of our brains.

It is in this field of battle that Popular Art must situate itself. All the Arts. We have to be *Allies* in this war against the fascism of the uni-vocal discourse.

The adepts of economic globalisation seek monopoly – cinematographic, phonographic, monopoly of all the means of communication by which they can impose their ideas and desires, making us believe that these are our own ideas and desires. We must impose a different Globalisation on them: we are Subjects not Objects!

The theatre is also a means of communication, albeit more complex than the simple radio news service. Every form of communication possesses its own means – some enlighten their interlocutors and help them to develop their perceptions of the world; others create fear.

Fear is a potent weapon which makes the viewers vulnerable: stuck in front of the screen, they are incapable of penetrating it, of taking action, of counter-attacking, of defending themselves. They are immobilised like rabbits caught in the glare of headlights.

Violence on television has nothing to do with art, and everything to do with terrorism, whose primary goal is to create general insecurity, creating imaginary or real focuses of danger, whilst hiding its origins, seeding a formless dread: where will the mortal blow come from? From what darkness, from what ill-lit recess? Where is the executioner hiding? Who will be the next victim? Why?

In the Greek tragic system, *Empathy* came about through the binomial[19] of Fear and Pity. Fear, because the catastrophe could happen to any of us – we were like the hero, whose misfortune we understood and knew to be foreseeable and ineluctable; Pity, because we admired his virtues. In Hollywood filmography, of a terrorist nature, *Empathy* comes about through Fear and Horror; the unexpected, the surprise, when all is possible even the impossible, even without cause. Through Fear and Horror, the worst, most evil ideas can be implanted into the inert audience. Empathy falsified transforms itself to docile Mimicry.

In Tragedy, the physical violence is carried out off-stage: Oedipus plucks out his eyes, off-stage; Medea would never murder her children before the frenetic applause of a gawping audience, munching on popcorn. But as for her *reasons*, these were present on stage. They danced in front of the Greek audiences who were respected as intelligent people, not treated like the rabid spectators of a bloody Thai boxing match.

Coercive system though it was, Greek tragedy respected the intelligence and stimulated thought. It could, as in the case of Euripides, provoke debate and the questioning of society and its values. Greek tragedy was the ballet of ideas, not a shambles of stray bullets!

Hollywood films have only one theme, i.e. that right belongs to the mighty who are always on the side of reason, reason being Good in its crusade against Evil – and Evil being those who think differently.

This ethically bankrupt trash, dumped onto our innocent neurons, feeds its poison gradually into our lived lives, affecting vulnerable viewers' subsequent reception of information. We cannot be shocked in the face of

Columbine-type[20] crimes which have been presaged and promoted by this type of cinema, nor can we forget that New York's Twin Towers were destroyed in a film fiction before they were filmed in flames in the real tragedy.[21]

Even the films which do not show explicit brutality – for instance, the light comedy with the happy ending – introduce into our heads the habits, customs and even the manners of speech of the citizens of their countries – along with dress styles, modes of work and play, relationship etiquettes, uses of money, moral options and reasons for living.

At the World Trade Organisation, some countries defend the so-called *cultural exception*, not because they defend Culture, but because, through it – in the form of cinema, music, videos, CDs, DVDs and other industries – business can foist its products on the viewer, through the image.

I am not speaking against that healthy species of business which satisfies the needs of the buyer – the delights of the open street market, of which I am an unconditional fan – but rather of that unwholesome brand of business which creates *unnecessary necessities*, invading our homes through television, radio, the papers, by telephone and on the internet – creating addiction.

Business has never been so invasive and so clamorous – long gone are the times when I was thrilled to hear the call of the basket-laden fishmonger, bawling out the virtues of his fresh prawns and singing the praises of his whiting.

The Aesthetics of the Oppressed is part of our struggle against this daily invasion.

9 METAPHOR AS TRANSLATION[22] OR TRANS-SUBSTANTIATION

Metaphor, in its broadest sense as *translation*, includes all symbolic languages, among them the Word, the Parable and the Allegory. It includes all the Arts which *represent* – rather than *reproduce* – realities. The Visual Arts use line, volume and colour; music uses sound and silence; dance, the musical body in motion.

The *aesthetic neurons* are those that process, jointly, ideas and emotions, memories and imagination, senses and abstractions. When these neurons are activated by new stimuli, the creation of Metaphor is activated. All Metaphors are Translations or Transubstantiations, i.e. the creations of new realities.

The human being is the only animal capable of creating Metaphors. The more it 'metaphorises', the more human it becomes. All the arts are Metaphors and only human beings are artists.

CTO-Rio Community Group: **Periferia em Ação**
Forum Theatre Play: **A Descoberta de Trancinha**
Subject: **Teenage pregnancy**
Directed by: **Roni Valk**
Photographer: **Carola Pagani (AFAB)**
FESTEL (Legislative Theatre Festival 2005 – Rio de Janeiro, Brazil)

Without an autonomous metaphoric activity – which is what the Aesthetics of the Oppressed seeks to develop – the intelligence is paralysed and the individual once again approaches the condition of hominid, where his evolution began! A long time back.[23]

I insist that hominids and animals were not, and still are not, capable of metaphorising activities; they are not capable of transcribing the reality which surrounds them and into which they have been thrust, into any other forms. The endless imperatives of the communication media promote this retrogression[24] to primitive states.

10 CROWNS OF NEURON CIRCUITS

The Crowns presented here are a *hypo-thesis*, i.e. less than a thesis. I can present no strict proofs of their existence, any more than a neuroscientist could present proofs of their non-existence.

Si non é vero, é bene trovato![25]

I give the name Crown to this system, taking my inspiration from the Royal Crowns that unified feuding clans in the Middle Ages, forming States. The

King submitted the barons, princes, counts, and other nobles to his rule, within a greater structure, the Kingdom, which incorporated them all.

The penetration of new sensory information into the Cortex, through the thalamus, and the cerebral circulation of abstract messages and concrete emotions, can take a fluid, harmonious, integrative form, enabling new circuits to form, which interlace, creating rich and complex *networks*, containing yet more neuron circuits.

But it can happen, with information that is particularly imperative or dogmatic, that in the circuits to which it gravitates, these networks harden, becoming opaque and compacted – turning into structures which, though internally coherent, refuse dialogue with new circuits external to themselves, impeding the arrival of new information which conflicts with that already existing in their own classification.

Examples of these *Crowns* are to be found in all forms of religious extremism, founded on the existence of internally coherent systems of Revelations and Dogmas which, even when absurd and implausible, are never questioned. These *Crowns* become aggressive and destructive in relation to other *Crowns* – other extremisms or fundamentalisms – or indeed towards any new information with which they differ.

They impede the free flow of Reason. As imperatives, they reject subjunctives.

The fervour of the fanatical sports fan, the idolatrous adoration of any person or institution, political sectarianism, allegiance to drug-trafficking gangs or Montague-and-Capulet-type clans – all these, even when there are also other social and economic reasons for them, are concrete examples of such *Crowns*, formed by the constant repetition of the same information with the same content, and by the acceptance of the same never-questioned values.

If the orations of an extremist religion – or by the extremists of any religion – were delivered only once every three or four months, these *Crowns* would not form. Since these orations are served up several times a day, they do form. If a football team only played a match once every six months, there would be no hooligans – as games are played twice a week, no time is left for the Subject to think other thoughts. If confrontation between gangs was accidental or sporadic, the result of a chance encounter in the street, dialogue would be possible. Since they go head-to-head every day, it is not.

Constant repetition leads to the production of *Crowns* which are refractory and aggressive. This condition on its own is not sufficient to cause this outcome, but it is a necessary part of the equation!

Crowns involve several regions of the brain. According to the theory of Hughlings-Jackson (1835–1911) some cerebral activities, such as those of the optic nerve, are fairly simple whilst others, like thought, involve the structuring of an immense quantity of simple elements.

Let us not forget that the brain is an ecological system where everything is interlinked, and not a computer hard disk.

11 AESTHETIC NEURONS

When, in relation to a given subject, Science has neither a precise explanation nor unquestionable knowledge, the way is open for poetic interpretation.

Besides neurons specialised in only one activity, there are also others that accumulate diverse functions within the circuits which include them, and are capable of receiving and transmitting physical sensations and profound emotions, complex ideas, words and symbols. These neurons and circuits are found mainly in the cortex and the thalamus, which are the most human parts of the human brain.

With apologies in advance to the neuroscientists, I want to baptise them 'Aesthetic Neurons', because such is the function of Aesthetics, through sensory stimuli, to reveal reason and produce emotion. These neural circuits have the capacity to perceive the world in its relation between the Singular and the Set, relativising it and discovering its logic.

Dostoyevsky wrote that 'Only Beauty will save the world', a phrase which we could translate to: 'Only Aesthetics can enable us to attain the truest and most profound comprehension of the world and society'.

Synapses are the meeting points between neurons, by means of *neurites* – comprised of *axons* which transmit, and *dendrites*, which receive: gentle arms which embrace each other, surfaces where information circulates – image, sound, word, pleasure and pain, memory, dialogues. That this can happen is thanks to chemical processes and electric stimuli.

The synapses multiply and diversify, in proportion to the stimulation they receive.[26] The more we know, the more our capacity to know grows. The more I apply myself to painting, the more I discover how to use a paintbrush, as if I were a painter. The more I apply myself to singing, the more I realise the range of my voice, as if I were a singer. The more I make my words dance on the page or out of my lips, the more I learn to love them, as if I were a poet. By doing, I will be painter, poet and singer. I am them.

Understanding, knowing by experience and experimenting expand my capacity to recognise, to apprehend and to learn. They expand beyond the bounds of my enquiry and bring me face to face with that which I was not even seeking. 'I don't seek: I find!' said Picasso. We are doing the same when, in pursuit of that goal, we dedicate ourselves to seeing what we are looking at, to listening to what we are hearing, to feeling what we touch, to writing what we think. We are all Picassos, each to our own degree . . . and in our own way.

12 VOLUME, TERRITORY AND THE INSIGNIA OF POWER

The stone, being inanimate, occupies a space in the world identical to its volume. Plants, being living things, grow and need more territory than the equivalent of their volume alone: trees, though immobile, nourished by earth and rain, spread shadows on the ground where the grass won't grow – ground which thus becomes part of the territory of the tree, greater than the volume of its body alone. In its leafy top, the tree's branches and leaves imprison space; its roots invade a greater area of the ground than the sum of their volumes.

Animals, being living things that move, fight for even greater space. Some, like dogs and wolves, mark their territories with scent, urinating so that it is known to whom that space belongs – they could empty their whole bladders on a single post or tree-trunk, but they prefer to use several posts or trunks to demarcate their space. Others achieve the same by sound: the lion roars, since he wouldn't be much of a lion if he went round urinating on posts with his leg cocked; tigers growl, cats hiss, the cock crows, the falcon screeches, the panther basks, the dove coos, the hyena laughs, the snake hisses and the ostrich booms.

Animals *privatise* space which belongs to all, and privatised space excludes: this is *my* house, *my* yard, *my* estate – it is not *your* house, *your* yard, *our* land. Animals need space to exist – territory. Thus the struggle begins, be it violent or subtle, for the space which becomes property – extensions of the body of the owner, whether lion or landowner. What happens in the forests and on the savannahs with wild animals, happens in Brazil with farmers who occupy federal lands, and on all stock exchanges with financial speculation: money is power, and power buys everything, starting with space.

Humans beings also use their senses to extend the limits of their territory. More than the ears or the nose, human beings use the eyes: the image. *All human societies are visual spectacles*, with the other senses assisting.[27] The thing that changes, with the march of History, is not the spectacular character of society: it is the means by which that spectacle is produced.

Our technologically sophisticated societies – which use electric light, radio, cinema and computers – give the impression that only they are spectacle, or that spectacle was born with them. In truth, in order to realise *its* spectacle, each society uses the means at its disposal, just as the dog uses its urine.

Our societies are *spectacular* in the aesthetic sense of the word, because they are based on power relations, and power demands signs and rituals. As power is abstract before being exercised, pure potential before the act, it requires concretion in order to be recognised at first sight and sound, in order to be feared and respected. It requires palpable insignia – made out of signals, signs and symbols[28] – well-structured rituals, conscious or unconscious.

Louis XIV awoke every morning in front of an audience chosen from his favourites at court, who waited anxiously to applaud his first matinal yawn, to the soothing sounds of lute and harpsichord, in fine compositions by Lully.

These nobles fought for the monarch's preference, dressing in robes appropriate for such a ceremony and applauding heartily with sweaty palms. The spectacle shows not only the pre-eminence of the monarch, its protagonist, but the whole hierarchy of power from the most powerful to the lowliest servants each structured in their specific rituals. All must play out their roles. Even naked, the King is always invested with pomp, dressed in imaginary silk and splendours.

The carriage was invented as a means of transport, but the carriage which carries kings and queens – if that were its only utility – would be much more efficiently replaced by a small popular car of two or three horse power, instead of those four or six comely animals of flesh and bone. The carriage is a symbol of power, of ancient hierarchy and eternal tradition. The fact that it transports people is secondary.

Insignia, which by their presence individualise their possessor as someone superior and powerful, are at the same time also *Images of Absence*. The royal crown makes us perceive our smallness – our heads are uncrowned! The King's crown un-crowns us. It shows his power and our weakness. Insignia show where power resides, and denounce us as non-possessors of this power: we are subjects, vassals, or slaves.

This is made explicit in the structure of all spectacles: when we see them, we understand everything, even if unconsciously, and we behave according to the place we occupy.

The greatest humiliation a soldier can suffer is when they take his medals from him in front of his regiment of medal-less soldiers: return to point zero.

These days, our spectacles tend not to be as full of artifice and ingenuity as those deployed by Louis; but still our kings show off their crowns, the pope his mitre, the general his stars, and the ladies of the courts of the bourgeoisie their jewels and plastic surgery.

Bokassa, the dictator of the Central African Republic,[29] though already in possession of uni-personal discretionary power, exercised by means of an

CTO-Rio Community Group: Maré Arte
Forum Theatre Play: A Maré da Vida
Subject: Domestic Violence
Directed by: Geo Britto
Photographer: Adriana Medeiros
Public presentation in a Community – Rio de Janeiro, Brazil

extremely bloody army, liked to present himself swathed in leopard-skin, and adorned with the precious stones once plentiful in his country. He demanded to be crowned Emperor for Life in the presence of foreign dignitaries. Covetous of such wealth, many came to the festivities and left sparkling.

Spectacle is not confined to a fifteenth birthday party at which the young woman dances her first waltz with her father, or the dance of the commoner Angelica with the Prince in Visconti's *The Leopard*, which opens the doors of nobility to her, or the marriage ceremony of a bride all dressed in white; nor is it only when the president of the Republic lays wreaths on the tomb of the Unknown Soldier, or a new road is officially opened. *Spectacle* is not just these moments of extravagance and pomp; it also embraces the hearty family Sunday lunch, where people eat and talk according to established rules, as in any piece of theatre.

Spectacle has the function of revealing who is who, as if planting a legend on the brow of each protagonist or supernumerary.[30]

The appearance of any citizen on the cover of a magazine, or in a society column or a sports page, or on a TV programme – which are all spectacular forms, static or dynamic – can give anyone, however 'insignificant' they may be, a power corresponding to the status the media confers on them – which lasts till the next edition of the paper. The media are, at one and the same time, a source of information and of validation of those that parade in their pages or on their screens: sources of power, like the crown or the mitre.

The extraordinary hypnotic power of TV is raised to paroxysm by the movement of the image. Any movement is attractive because of its unpredictability – all movement creates *suspense*. Even in the cot, the baby's gaze is attracted to anything that moves; movement is one of the healthy ways of developing its attention.

TV utilises this biological fact: as a general rule its images do not stay on the screen more than a few fleeting seconds. Not to allow the viewers to see an image they are looking at is a basic principle of televisual hypnosis.

Another unpredictable is TV's sound, designed to catch one unawares, to startle.

It is curious that the cinema, which in times of yore was calm and tranquil, no longer permits Antonionis: it has absorbed the vertigo of TV's velocity. The small screen is seen in the illuminated living room, where spectators are carrying out noisy activities in parallel (dining, playing cards, talking at the top of their voices . . .). On the big screen, this hysteria of image would not be necessary since the milieu is a darkened room in which, at worst, the distraction is only the crackle of popcorn and the slurp of unhealthy beverages.

TV is made to sell products and ideas, the latter through the insidious mechanism of *empathy*, which makes us suspend our critical faculty and our need to be active so that, immobilised in body and soul, we are at the mercy of the shallow thought, the worthless language, coarse and hollow, the consumerist mentality. Even in the comedies our laughter is programmed and obligatory: canned laughter, played in the background, informs us that such and such a scene or phrase is funny and, by mechanical means, shows us when we should laugh, even if we don't find it funny.

It is not always the case that the format of these programmes foredooms them. The idea of the reality show, in itself, is not totally bad. If, instead of vacuous and mediocre people, the producers invited Noam Chomsky, Arthur Miller, Amy Goodman and Michael Moore – to cite only North American intellectuals – to stay in a room for twenty-four hours exchanging ideas, I would not sleep for those twenty four hours – my eyes would be glued to the screen. The participants themselves would place their own boundaries on their behaviour, which would prevent it from becoming what such shows have usually been – i.e. permissive sessions of repugnant voyeurism. This would be a meeting of intellects rather than of aberrations.

A paradox: TV is turning into the absolute truth, and reality into fiction, until it is reinstated as truth by the evening news.

At the end of the last decade, in the centre of Rio de Janeiro, there was an assault on a bus, with hostages taken, which lasted five hours and was filmed in its entirety by television. A young woman confessed that, when she passed by the area and saw what was happening in front of her eyes, she dashed straight home, and turned on the television to be sure that what she had witnessed in the flesh was true.

The means applied to the realisation of the spectacle change with the culture of each people, but its function is the same. Less technological, indigenous Brazilians use coloured plumage which they exhibit at their festivals or when they are preparing for war. Some use flattened spheres – their mitre and crown – with which they perforate their lips, lending them a fearsome aspect. Everyone dances respectfully, in turn, in search of a place in the structure of power, which proximity to the *cacique* (chief) confers. In a different context, it is the same as the nobles of Louis XIV, awaiting his awakening.

13 THE THREE LEVELS OF PERCEPTION

To live, to exercise our power and occupy our territory, we humans, and animals of all kinds, need to perceive the world in which we live. This perception takes place on three levels:

1 *Information – the receptive level*: light is reflected onto objects, passes through the crystalline lens of my eyes, stimulates my retina which informs the optic nerve, which makes this electrochemical information circulate till it reaches that region of the brain which will make me see what is in front of me. I receive the message. This information is not archived – on the contrary, it inter-relates with other neural circuits. The same occurs with the other senses.

2 *Knowledge and Tactical Decision-Making – the more active level*: the individual relates the new information to similar or complementary information she has received before, and takes reactive decisions.

On these two levels, humans and animals are the same: both decide, react. In some, the decisions are instinctive or biological. Mice raised in the laboratory, who have never seen the face or colour of a cat, and are unacquainted with its nature – evil, from the mice's point of view – flee terrified when they detect the feline smell: even without knowing its enemy, the mouse reacts biologically and is repelled by the smell.

In the human being, Knowledge is accompanied by a subjective valuation, which can lead to error. In us, Information and Knowledge raise us to the third level, as in this example:

I open the door of my house and see a tiger, escaped from the circus: my optic nerve registers its presence – I receive the *Information*! Excellent! My senses are functioning. Happy me.

The tiger approaches and information continues to arrive with electrochemical neuronal precision: twenty metres, ten, five. The tiger roars, and I hear its roar: my auditory nerve is activated, bravo! I am even happier with the perfect functioning of two of my senses.

The tiger opens its enormous mouth – my olfactory glands are activated and I sense its hot breath! I am content; the information is correct. I have been well informed by my eyes, my ears and my nose – what a piece of work I am! The tiger opens his gullet, grinning like a Cheshire cat! Marvellous, I can see everything, so close am I to its razor teeth. Wonderful, all the information I need is coming through to me perfectly . . . until the tiger clamps his jaws down tight on me and unhappily I receive no further sensory information. What a pity!

If my psychic process were to stop at this sensory information level, I would be hungrily gobbled up without further ado. But, happily, I had already stored in my brain many more important pieces of information about tigers and, at the *Knowledge* level, I already knew that the tiger was dangerous. I knew that I could bar the door and lock it. I knew that I had legs, so I could run and take refuge on the top floor. I knew that I could save myself, like the mouse fleeing the cat.

As a human, however, I am not necessarily reduced to flight. I can take creative decisions, strategic and not merely tactical decisions. I can seek other solutions. I can invent, choose what to do. I keep a revolver in my drawer and I can kill the tiger. I go up to the second floor, open the drawer, put my hand inside and . . .

3 *Ethical Consciousness – the human level*: this level is exclusive to the human being. It consists of giving meaning and value to the decisions we take. I interrogate myself. This is the level of doubt and of ethically justified choice.

Should I kill the tiger? After all, it is malnourished, starving – the economic crisis has reduced its rations! The tiger only wants to eat me to satiate its hunger, it bears me no ill will: for it to eat person or animal is as natural as it is for the piranha to devour a cow.[31] I could save myself but, if I let it go, the tiger could eat my neighbour's son, who is in the yard playing with the tricycle he got for Christmas – the meat on the little boy would be tenderer than me.

Do I dial 999? Do I throw my writing table at the tiger's head to startle it? Do I scream?

This third level is Ethical: it accords values to each act and projects the human being in his *actions* into the future, rather than merely dwelling on his *reactions* in the present.

It is creative: it requires the invention of alternatives. It is on this ethical level that a Forum Theatre session should operate: good ideas are not enough; they need to be ethically justified. It is not enough to work with ideas that already exist: we need to invent.

In our theatre work, it is important to extend and amplify all the levels of our perception, especially the Ethical, so that our choices may be conscious – as in 'con-science', *with knowledge* – of the possibilities that exist or can be created, in each situation: there is always choice!

14 THE NECESSITY FOR THE AESTHETICS OF THE OPPRESSED

The Aesthetics of the Oppressed – which I want to become an inseparable part of the Theatre of the Oppressed – is essential, in so far as it produces a new form of understanding, helping the subject to *feel* and, through the senses and not just the intelligence, to *understand* social reality.

The Aesthetics of the Oppressed embraces more than simple perception; it aims at enabling fuller knowledge and placing in front of the person any ethical decisions to be made. It seeks to produce emotional and intellectual stimuli, encapsulating the symbolic language of the word and the *signalétique* language of the senses.

CTO-Rio Community Group: **Corpo EnCena**
Forum Theatre Play: **Ser Doutor, João. Não é mole não!**
Subject: **Peer pressure on urban youth**
Directed by: **Olivar Bendelak**
Photographer: **Declev Dib Ferreira**
Public presentation in a Community – Rio de Janeiro, Brazil

Theatre is the most natural form of learning, and the most primal, since the child learns to live by means of theatre, playing, acting characters – and, through the other arts, looking at himself and painting, singing and dancing.

It is true that this learning, this *apprenticeship*, utilises the prevailing social structures and ethical values of each society; to avoid the passive acceptance of this society as it is, there is the Theatre of the Oppressed – whose mode is subjunctive and not imperative – questioning values and structures.

The child must learn to live in society and also to question it.

Theatre games involve a synthesis of Discipline and Liberty. Every game has clear rules which must be obeyed, but, within the bounds of obedience to the rules, invention is free and necessary.

Every game is an apprenticeship for life; the theatre game is an apprenticeship for social life. The games of the Theatre of the Oppressed are an apprenticeship for citizenship. Without discipline, there is no social life. Without liberty, there is no life. Games are metaphors for social life.

As a member of the MST (*Movimento dos Trabalhadores Rurais Sem-Terras* – Landless Rural Workers Movement) put it: 'The Theatre of the Oppressed is wonderful because it enables people to learn everything that they already knew'. You learn, *aesthetically* – it broadens the knowing and launches the knower in search of further knowledge.

Let us learn to learn and learn to discover!

We have to activate our *Aesthetic Neurons* by means of the *subjunctive* teaching of Images – looking and seeing; of Sound and of Music – hearing and listening; of the Word – poetry and narrative; and, in all this aesthetic and social activity, we have to seek our own Ethical orientation, the first element of which should be *To multiply what has been learnt.*

The stimulus which happens in one area of the brain propagates itself to the surrounding areas: chords in music develop visual potentialities, not just auditory ones. Chess champions study classical music to imagine creative strategies. Einstein played the violin when he could make no progress with his mathematical labours, and returned to mathematics when he found the necessary stimulus in the chords of his violin. Music is the sound of mathematics. It is mathematics refined into sounds.

The Aesthetic Neurons are the most important of all the neurons of the nervous system, according to the hypothesis that, within them, the senses coexist with reason, the concrete with the abstract. Aesthetic perception incorporates reason and emotion, judgements and values, not just sensations![32]

In the same way as sport expands the potentialities of the body, art expands those of the mind.

The seeds of this Aesthetic Project are already in the original Arsenal of the Theatre of the Oppressed – the Image Games and Techniques are already Visual Arts – all that is lacking is their extrapolation into the concrete work of art. The Rhythm Games and Techniques are already Music – all that is lacking is their transformation into songs and symphonies. Improvisation already produces Literature: all that is lacking is their solidification into poems and narratives.

Beware: this is not a matter of teaching *solfeggio* or forcing people to sing the second part of the National Anthem – a martyrdom inflicted on me in my infancy[33] – rather we are talking about developing the musicality that we all possess already.

This is not about organising Supplementary Art Classes to make good the shortcomings of childhood teaching; or teaching drawing, colour and line to sketch Greek statues or nude models better, as in the faculty. It is about helping people to broaden their sensibilities, their artistic tendencies and their embryonic knowledge.[34]

Our quest is for Beauty, like any other artist. The Beauty which is, as Hegel wrote, the shining of the truth that becomes perceptible through the senses. The truth that is hidden behind appearances. But this Hegelian truth is essentially the revelation of God Himself – while our truth is invented by humans, a Human Ethics. Ethics is a human invention and a conscious desire, not a Revelation.

We seek the Beauty hidden in the heart of each and every citizen, since every citizen is an artist – each in his or her own way: even though some may not be capable of creating an *Aesthetic Product* which enlightens all of us, all are capable of developing an *Aesthetic Process* which enriches themselves.

We pursue Culture, not only to understand and enjoy Culture that is foreign to us – Erudition, which is the knowledge of other Cultures! – but to develop our own identity. We are what we do, and if we make or do only what others have invented, we will be a copy of others, not ourselves.

The knowledge of the culture of other people and other times, or of finished works of art, is important for all of us, however far removed it may seem. The young people of a poor community who learn to dance the waltz with Austrian rigour, or a fine minuet with French elegance, are learning something and are being aesthetically stimulated, although the 'nobility and equilibrium of the movements'[35] of this dance have nothing to do with their daily lives. If they mount a faithful staging of a play by Molière, or learn to play a Chopin nocturne with equal fidelity, clearly this alone can broaden the horizons of their perception, and this learning is wonderful.

We must be conscious that no *structure* of dance, music or theatre is innocent or empty: all contain the world vision of the person who makes them – i.e. that person's ideology – which, through the artistic form, is assimilated and incorporated by anyone who practises them.

At the times of Chopin and Strauss, European peasants didn't dance waltzes or minuets, a pastime only compatible with the leisure of the rich. It is great to know how to dance Minuets and Waltzes – and even greater to discover the dance our own body is capable of creating.[36]

Unless we create our own culture, we will be obedient and servile to other cultures. And when we are creating our own culture, other cultures can only be beneficial to us, expanding our sensibility. The fact of being who I am, when I know who I am, does not stop me from admiring what others do. Unless I know who I am, I will be a copy.

The Aesthetics of the Oppressed is a project about helping the oppressed to discover Art *by discovering their art and, in the act, discovering themselves*; to discover the world, *by discovering their world and, in the act, discovering themselves*, instead of receiving information from the media, TV, radio, foreign music, etc., to create their own artistic metaphors of their own world.

15 THE SUBJUNCTIVE METHOD

The theatre usually conjugates reality in the *Present Tense of the Indicative Mood* – 'I do'. TV and advertising use the *Imperative Mood* – 'Do!' In the Theatre of the Oppressed, reality is conjugated in the *Subjunctive Mood*, in two tenses: the *Past Imperfect* – 'what if I were doing that?' – or the *Future* – 'what if I were to do this?'

In our work with peasants fighting for land to cultivate, or with young people undergoing punishment in correctional establishments, in poor communities, with people with physical or mental disabilities, with factory workers or domestic servants, or whoever – we have to be *Subjunctive*.

Everything should be 'what if', because everything can come to be.

Subjunctive – that's the word! The Subjunctive Theatre must be accompanied by the *Legislative Theatre*[37] so that the knowledge acquired during the theatrical work can be extrapolated into laws and juridical actions, or by Invisible Theatre, to intervene directly in reality. Or by the prosecution of oppressor-offenders to get some moral and/or financial reparation for the victims or to bring to people's attention the issue you want to deal with, or by a Concrete Action, which changes things in the immediate future, plunging straight into reality, like a workers' strike, the occupation of a piece of unproductive land, etc.

The Subjunctive Method is the reinstatement of doubt as the seed of certainties. It is the comparison, discovery and counterposition of possibilities, not of a single certainty set against another, which we have in reserve. It is the construction of diverse models of future action for a particular given situation, enabling their evaluation and study.

We should never say, 'Do this or that!', but rather, 'If we did this or that, how would it be?' Even when the participants in our programmes do something really fine and admirable, we should still ask for more alternatives: what if it was different, how would that be?

16 THE METAPHOR: HUMANS AND HOMINIDS

In the Aesthetics of the Oppressed we concentrate our efforts and focus our attention on the creation of conditions in which the oppressed can develop fully their metaphoric world – their thought, their imagination and their capacity to symbolise, to dream, and to create parables and allegories, which allow them to see, from a certain distance, the reality they want to modify – without diminishing their participation in the social concrete world. We cannot see the real if our noses are glued to it – some aesthetic distance is necessary.

Alongside the sensible, signifying world, we want to develop the world of the signified.

The transformation of the artisan, he or she who creates the whole piece, into the worker – he or she who does a specific task without having any power over the final product, like the metal worker who feeds the nut into the bolt without knowing if the final product will be a car or a tractor – takes from the artisan, transformed into worker, the greater part of his capacity to imagine. It takes away the artist that exists in every artisan.

The hominids transformed themselves into human beings when they developed imagination, symbolic language, metaphor – when they invented the word, cave painting, dance, theatre. The human being creates what Plato called the *World of Perfect Ideas* – non-existent in the sensible world and exclusively human, in counterposition to the imperfect existing world of sensible realities.

Socrates had already established the concept of *Logos* (not the isolated event or phenomenon, but its meaning, the concept which embraces all the facts or phenomena of the same nature), on which Plato based his theory.

Taking some poetic licence – always useful in these circumstances – we can say that dance is the *Logos* of movement, just as music is the *Logos* of sound, and theatre the *Logos* of Life. Morality is the geometry of human behaviour; Ethics, the dream of perfection.

Aristotle upheld the idea that perfection was contained in every being – it was not a world apart, disconnected from the real. It was the real in movement, the search for something perfect, non-existent.

The hominids, as they transformed into human beings, made the split between brain and mind, material and spirit. The physical, anatomical brain, under the pressure of new intellectual necessities, developed the Cortex, where thoughts, evaluations, art, science, alternatives – in short, the subjective, abstract and metaphorical world – are processed. That's how things happen: necessity creates a new reality.

That reminds me of a sentiment most heard from the mouths of physiotherapists on *use and disuse*: that all parts of the body develop when used and when in disuse, they atrophy. The brain is part of the body and the rule of *use and disuse* applies to it too.

Art is the most human characteristic of the human being: it is his or her capacity to recreate the world. When the first inhabitants of the caves began to paint outlines of bison and other animals on the walls of their caves they were moving towards a pictorial Metaphor. We should not see them with modern eyes. They were not *decorating* their *apartments* by hanging pictures on the walls – on the contrary, they were effecting the Metaphor of recreating the animals, as concrete and threatening as they seemed to them in real life, in another context: painting. In this way, they could study them, since they needed to kill and eat them. They could also use these images for their magic rituals.

Art is Metaphor. Metaphor, in its broadest meaning, is any translation. It is the transposition of something, which exists within one context, to another context. Painting and sculpture are metaphors because, by the very

CTO-Rio Community Group: Pirei na Cenna
Forum Theatre Play: É melhor prevenir que remédio dar (Prevention is better than cure)
Subject: (Mental health service users' rights)
Directed by: Claudia Simone
Photographer: Carola Pagani (AFAB)
FESTEL (Legislative Theatre Festival 2005 – Rio de Janeiro, Brazil)

elements which they use – paint, canvas, metal, clay, etc. – they are already distancing themselves from the original reality, creating another, the similar and different. The same thing happens with cinema. The very act of filming is already metaphoric.

The naturalistic theatre tends to stick to original reality. Some styles, however, by their very presentation as image, foster this vigorous aesthetic and metaphoric distancing: the Japanese Noh and Kabuki, the Indian Kathakali, the Italian Commedia del'Arte, Greek tragedy, the story-tellers from our North-East, etc. Only we humans are capable of these translations. We are the only metaphoric animal.

This *leap*, from physical brain to consciousness, is as important and as mysterious as that other *leap*, from inanimate material to life. Equally mysterious and important is the leap from sensory perception to sadness or joy, from sensation to emotion, as mysterious as the process of thinking, which arises from this conjunction.

These mysterious leaps contradict Leibnitz, German philosopher of the eighteenth century, for whom nature *non facit saltus*.[38] Yes it does.

These mysteries, together with the idea of the two Infinites – the Greater Infinite and the Lesser Infinite, the without and the within – are the supreme and ultimate mysteries of existence which we will never understand. For the time being. The last mysteries, until the next ones!

In our societies, with the end of better oppressing the oppressed, the oppressors seek to reduce the symbolic life of the oppressed, their imag-ination, consigning them to mechanised work in which they are replaceable by any other – their names become numbers. Quality turns into quantity, and the human being is robotised.

The leisure time of the oppressed, when they have any, is populated with images – from the media, from religions, sometimes extremist, and from others – which aim to retransform humans into hominids, countering the evolution of the species, *Panem et Circenses* – Bread and Circuses! – to use the words of the satirical poet Juvenal (AD 42–125) describing the Romans in their decadence, or *Pan y Toros* (Bread and Bulls), as the Spanish say.

In every human being there squats a hominid: let us not fall into temptation. Let us be metaphoric – let us be people!

The Aesthetics of the Oppressed aims at the liberation and fortification of metaphoric activity, of symbolic languages, of intelligence and sensitivity. It aims at the expansion of the perception that we have of the world. This is done through the Word, the Image, and the Sound, guided by a Humanist Ethic.

THE PRACTICAL REALISATION: THE PROMETHEUS PROJECT

From the beginning of this essay we have been talking about naming *Sets* – so we name this aesthetic set: the *Prometheus Project*, in homage to the Titan who taught humans how to make fire, which he had stolen from the gods, who wanted it all for themselves.

The *Project* aims to develop all Aesthetic forms of perception of reality, in the members of the groups of oppressed people with whom we are working. There are four main approaches:

1 THE WORD

Our objective is not to transform every citizen into a writer of airport best-sellers, but to enable all to be master or mistress of a major human invention: the word, the symbolic language.

Words, in order to be symbols – a symbol being a thing which stands in the place of another – need to be charged with the hopes, desires, needs and life experiences of each citizen. The word is one thing, and the meaning that we give it is another, the two not always coinciding.

We know that every word comes loaded with the desires of its sender. We also know that every receiver has their own structures of reception. When a housemaid hears the word *Maria*, the appellation often given to a housemaid by her employers, whatever her given name, this word comes associated with an order: Maria, make the lunch; Maria, do the washing; Maria, clean the house: Maria, do this, do that. *Maria* comes to be the forewarning of an order. And Maria becomes a soldier who listens and obeys.

When, however, Maria writes her own name because she has a lot to say about herself, she rediscovers herself and can associate her name, Maria, with love, with pleasure, with politics. To assume her name – and give her own values to it – is a way of reclaiming herself as subject. To write is a way of dominating the word, instead of being dominated by it.

In this Chapter of the project, there are three starting points:

THE THING WHICH HAS MADE THE STRONGEST IMPRES-SION ON ME IN RECENT YEARS – the participants are invited to write a short narrative about an intimate personal event, or, by contrast, an event of national interest, something it has been impossible to forget. In contrast to the Declaration of Identity (see below), where the subject is turned inwards to their internal world, this is an opportunity to reflect on the panoramic vision which each of us has of the world we live in. It is not enough just to tell the story – the participant must reveal in what particular, unique fashion this event made an impression on him or her, something personal. If the first attempt remains in the realm of mere narration, it must be insisted that the participant digs deep in his or her memory and reveals more subjective impressions. And then in the discussion, these personal impressions must be related back to the social and political significance of the event.

Suggestion: one interesting practice consists of sticking the texts that people have written up on the wall or passing them around those present, without saying who is the author of each one. After this, people are asked which text made most impression on them and why. Only then will we ask who wrote each text and invite its author to comment on the remarks made about his or her writing. Everyone should be free to intervene, sharing related stories and facts they know, trying to discover connections between them.

DECLARATIONS OF IDENTITY – each participant must declare who they are, in a few lines, three times, with three different recipients in mind: for instance, a loved one, a neighbour, the boss on whom their employment or function depends, the president of the country or another figure of authority. Some prefer to declare themselves to their cat or their dog, their garden, even their plate of food – any of which will also serve.

Each time that they declare who they are, as *our identity is also bestowed upon us by our relationship with others* – none of us is confined within ourselves – the writers discover identities which exist, which are indeed theirs, but in disuse or unsuspected. He or she discovers his or her own multiplicity and richness.

To undertake the Declaration of Identity is to dive deep within oneself. 'It is a way of giving us the courage to speak out loud what we write in silence', said a participant in one of our groups.

POETRY – each participant must write a poem, following their intuition. By way of stimulus, rather than rule, we can propose stages. The participant:

1 chooses a theme which moves them – an emotion is necessary. It can be the eyes of their loved one or a hole in their shoe, the smile of the new-born baby or the prices in the supermarket;
2 writes a page, with all the emotions and reflections their theme arouses; the lines must be shorter than the width of the paper;
3 eliminates the superfluous words, such as articles and adverbs ending in '-ly', which weigh down the lines; the art of writing well is the art of knowing what to cut;
4 organises the line in such a way as to create rhythm; they must read the text out loud, observing if their reading rolls with an internal rhythm;

5 if they want it to rhyme, the poets must replace the last words of each verse to achieve this effect, with the caveat that poetry doesn't have to rhyme;

6 the poem is born.

If this process does not get results, they can invent others. In art, rules are only suggestions, never imperative laws.

2 THE IMAGE

We must develop our capacity not only to hear, but also to see. The creation of images produced by ourselves rather than by nature or a machine, serves to show that the world can be re-created. The creation of Images of the world as we want it to be, is the best way to penetrate the future.

The participant intervenes to change reality, as when the cave painters painted bisons, bears and mammoths in their caves with the same intention. Though I have no eye-witness testimony I would swear that the rest of the cave dwellers gathered around the painter to study alongside him the ways of attacking these wild beasts; the painting stimulated mimicry, theatre, dance.

Painting and sculpture are ways of restructuring the world, of reinventing it. It is no surprise that painters and sculptors should feel god-like, since they remake and correct the world of the divinity.

The basic image activities should be:

PAINTING AND SCULPTURE – each group must produce a collective creation under the title *Human Being in Junk*, using elements of *clean rubbish* from their communities or places of work. Each sculpture must show one or more human figures at work, at leisure, in love, in dialogue or in solitude, as they wish.

Apart from *clean rubbish*, they can use glue, string, wire, wood, and other elements to hold the sculpture together. They must also make paintings on the same theme. This is the starting point and other subjects should be sought within the group's range of interests: work, home, the street, the future.

PHOTOGRAPHY – apart from the brain, the hands are the most human part of each of us. Somehow, they are the physical translation of our minds.

Each participant must take, or ask someone else to take, three photos of their hands or of the hands of people who work in the same profession, or live in the same community.

What are the hands doing? Are they working with a spade, grasping the steering wheel of a car, holding a broom, striking the keyboard of a

CTO-Rio Community Group: Artemanha
Forum Theatre Play: Vícios (Bad habits)
Subject: Substance abuse
Directed by: Helen Sarapeck and Flávio Sanctum
Photographer: Adriana Medeiros
FESTEL (Legislative Theatre Festival 2003 – Rio de Janeiro, Brazil)

computer or the keys of a piano? Caressing a face, or a glass, or a body? Washing plates, lashing out, or playing cards? Are they translating thoughts into gestures? Are they expressive or mechanised?

The photographer must take the photo their subject wants, which may not be the photo they would have chosen to take. The photographer brings to bear his or her technical knowledge of using the camera, so that the photo will reproduce what the participant desires.

Other subjects can be: oppression, the house where I live, family, the world, my work, my leisure. The subject is important, and still more important is the resultant dialogue about the images produced, the ways each image is perceived, the ideas which each image provokes, the memories, the desires.

RE-FORMING THE FORM – a well-known image is presented, like the national flag, the silhouette of a cold drink or an accident of geography (for instance, Rio de Janeiro's *Pão de Açúcar, Corvocado*), the logo of a fast food company, the shape of a football pitch, the profile of a city, an advertisement in which the body of a woman is associated with an alcoholic beverage, etc. The participants must remake it or transform it – colouring it, reshaping the lines, eliminating or adding lines and colours – in such a way as to give an opinion on that effigy and its meaning.

3 THE SOUND

Music is the form through which the human being relates with the Universe and its rhythms and random sounds. It is a form through which the human being relates to itself, to the rhythms of the heart and the breath, the circadian rhythms (sleep, hunger, etc.) and to the melody of the blood in the veins.

Music is the human being's contact with the heart and the Cosmos. For precisely this reason, economic power imprisons music in its festivals, its phonographic businesses, its distributors, etc., favouring always standardised rhythms which can be dominated by this power. Eighty per cent of the music which one hears on the radio has the mission of deadening the minds of its listeners. Hallucinatory rhythms have hallucination as their goal, this being one of the best ways of hiding oneself from oppressive reality.

In the Aesthetics of the Oppressed the goal is not to learn the rhythms which are played everywhere, but to rediscover and connect with our own internal rhythms, with the rhythms of nature, of work and of social life.

Starting from the games *The Image of the Hour, The Game of Professions, Masks and Rituals,* and others, the participants can choose any repetitive activity from their professional or day-to-day lives and transform it into dance:

1 the actors show in silence the repeated, mechanised – sometimes unconsciously – movements and gestures of their professional work or of a segment of their daily lives; it must be an activity which the participant's body is used to executing in a mechanical manner;

2 they amplify these gestures, eliminating the insignificant details, and magnifying the essentials. In this way, a sequence of essential movements is arrived at. Over a period of some time, they must execute these movements in a magnified way, then in a minimised way; in a very quick movement and in a slow movement, taking time to see and feel what the quotidian movement hides – to see and feel how each movement acts on their bodies, excites them, stimulates them or causes them pain or pleasure, *penetrating the unique* and not merely reproducing the obvious, even if the obvious is the point of departure. This movement must be the backbone of the dance to be constructed. All the rest of the movements must constantly refer back to it. The group can choose one, two or more of these internal rhythms – the important thing is that they feel it;

3 the actors must transform the movement into dance, introducing rhythm; the group must invent the music to go with this dance, whenever possible using instruments invented from objects in use in the places of work or in the group's community. All the musical instruments there are were made once by someone. They are not found ready-made in nature: so it follows that many others can be invented. Let's invent!

4 after they have a sequence of rhythmical gestures, they must imagine a scene in the life of these characters: an amorous liaison, petitioning for a salary increase, a marriage, a strike, a family gathering. The actors must tell the hidden story, using the gestures and rhythmical movements of their dance;

5 as a form of exercise to help the actors create the dance, the director must ask them in addition to perform their movements very slowly – now in slow motion, now fast forward; when there is sound, it should be as low as possible, scarcely audible, and then as loud as possible – always making sure the passage from one extreme to the other is executed gently, not in sudden jumps.

The participants should create rhythms and melodies starting from what they notice in their body in repose and in different daily activities, in the relationships between their body and the world. It is important to avoid known rhythms.

SYNAESTHESIA – this is the simultaneous perception by different senses, or the translation from one sense into another. For example, we have a presentiment of the taste of chocolate even when we see it from afar. We must ask the participants, when they see a picture or a photo that inspires them, to write a poem or a text. Or when reading a poem, to think of a piece of music. Or when they are listening to a piece of music, to paint the sounds which they hear.

CULTURE AND ERUDITION – all these suggestions have the goal of developing the individual creativity of each participant and their capacity to work in groups. Nevertheless, it is not our project to make a *tabula rasa* of the culture accumulated by Humanity, as if all that has been made to date was worth nothing. That would be nonsensical.

For this reason, we must offer our groups the possibility of getting to know our cultural sources, national and regional, as well as those of other countries and other times.

In terms of the Word, we have all our writers from the Portuguese invasions of the fifteenth century onwards, since very little survives of the oral indigenous literature prior to this. We have also a vast production of *cordel* literature,[39] poems written and sold in pamphlets of six to eight pages about legends or very recent events. And we have excellent modern writers.

In terms of Sound, Brazilian music continues in all its vigour, in spite of the predominance in our media of low-cost, easy-to-assimilate imported rhythms. Each one of our principal regions creates dozens of rhythms and dances, some under the influence of Europe, others home-grown.

In terms of Image, apart from our better known extraordinary modern painters, we have the art of our clay sculptors – indigenous people and people from the North-East. And we still have, to the amazement of the majority, wonderful cave art in the Piauí region: twenty thousand years ago they were already painting in our country on the walls of our caves.

Apart from our Culture, we must expose our groups to 'high art', created by other peoples in other times, from Bach to Beethoven, and to dialogues from the *Magic Flute* to the Andean flute. This dialogue will also be fertile.

4 THE ETHICS

The Theatre of the Oppressed is an *ethical theatre* and, in it, nothing can be done unless we know why and for whom it is being done. The participants of the *Prometheus Project* must know why they are doing what they are doing. The ethical significance of every action is as important as the action itself.

THE THEORY – we are not talking about giving classes on Ethics, but rather studying essential moments of Humanity when historic decisions or interpretations of the World, whether ethical or anti-ethical, were made through discussions, testimony, debates, etc. These include, for instance, the time of the pre-Socratic philosophers who revealed the disquiet of human beings in relation to the meaning of life, human relations and the substance of the Universe; the Spanish invasions of the sixteenth century in Central and South America, which resulted in the genocide of indigenous civilisations; the Bretton Woods Agreement which instituted the dollar as the universal currency; the Gulf War, the Iraq War, Vietnam.

THE PRACTICE: SOLIDARITY – the moral superiority of the fire brigade over the Military Police in Brazil, is owed to various factors, one of the most important being the content of the teachings that the foot soldiers of these two organisations receive. Military police officers learn to shoot, grab, beat, and destroy; firefighters, apart from putting out fires, learn first aid and how to save lives, to give service to the community. It is in the *doing* that the human being *makes him- or herself.*

This part of Ethics will be made up of practical lessons in solidarity which will be put into practice and not merely learnt! Each participant will have to collaborate concretely towards the achievement of some collective task or action proposed or being done by the community.

Today, many groups that practise TO in India under the umbrella of *Jana Sanskriti*, straight after each show in a community, ask what they can do to help that community, and then they do it. It forms part of their theatrical work.

SOLIDARY MULTIPLICATION – each group will have to organise other small groups to which they can transmit the learning, following the notion that *one only learns when one teaches*, in quest of the *Multiplicatory Effect.*

This is a scientific, neurological truth: in the act of learning, the individual mobilises the neurons necessary for the perception and retention of that which is learnt; in teaching, she mobilises neuron circuits of many areas. She expands and fixes her knowledge. She re-evaluates what has been learnt in the act of trying to explain it. In some languages, a single word is used to mean both 'teaching' and 'learning'; Welsh, for instance, has the word *dysgu*.

This is the initial project. For its results to be evaluated we will have to carry out work and experiments over a number of years, in the most diverse fields, in cities and countries where the Theatre of the Oppressed is used.

I hope that this will serve as a good point of departure.

Notes

1 The quality of the unique: 'The unicity we strive not to express, for that is impossible, but to designate by the nearest analogy', Coleridge, *OED*.

2 The forest is not contained in any of the trees of which it is comprised, but would not exist without them. The city is not any of its streets or squares, but, without them, there would

be no cities. The Portuguese poet Fernando Pessoa wrote: 'Perhaps it may be the Great Secret,/ That Great Mystery of which the false poets speak./ I saw that there is no Nature/ That Nature does not exist/ That there are mountains, valleys, plains/ That there are trees, flowers, grasses,/ That there are rivers and stones,/ (But) that there is no whole to which this belongs,/ That any real and genuine conjunction (of these) is a sickness of our ideas./ Nature is parts without a whole./ ... It was this that without thought or pause/ I realised must be the truth/ That all set out to find and do not find/ And that I alone, because I did not try to find it, found.' From *The Keeper of Sheep* (O Guardador dos Rebanhos) by Alberto Caeiro (heteronym of Fernando Pessoa).

('Talvez seja o Grande Segredo,/ Aquele Grande Mistério de que os poetas falsos falam./ Vi que não há Natureza/ Que Natureza não existe/ Que há montes, vales, planícies,/ Que há árvores, flores, ervas,/ Que há rios e pedras,/ Que não há um todo a que isso pertença,/ Que um conjunto real e verdadeiro/ É uma doença das nossas idéias./ A Natureza é partes sem um todo./ Foi isto o que sem pensar nem parar/ Acertei que devia ser a verdade/ Que todos andam a achar e que não acham/ E que só eu, porque a não fui achar, achei').

3 The Sets refer only to the sensory perception of the world and organise themselves into fictional, imaginary Structures, which constitute themselves by means of the intervention of the word and of symbols – of the grammatical word, as Lexicon and, above all, as Syntax. Structures are Sets of Sets, inter-related by analogy or complementarity: Moral Structures, Political Structures, Social, Family, Ritual, Behavioural, etc.

The structures sustain themselves by Power Relations, which play, in the human and animal field, the same role as the forces of the Universe (gravitational, electromagnetic, and those interactions called strong and weak, which occur in atomic nuclei). All human relations are structured by Power Relations in their various forms – political, social, psychological, cultural, charismatic, sexual, etc. – which determine values. These values, which are abstractions, determine concrete behaviours.

4 Cratilus was a disciple of Heraclitus, the Greek pre-Socratic philosopher, of the sixth to seventh centuries BC, who said that no one can enter the same river twice because, the second time, the waters will already be different from those that were passing by the first time – it will no longer be the same river. Cratilus went further than Heraclitus, saying that no-one can cross the same river even a single time, since the waters will always be in movement: what waters will the person who is crossing be entering?

I go further than Cratilus and ask: 'Who am I, the person crossing?'

5 The significations of the signifiers (the words) are different from the signification of the word together with the act of signifying. When I signify something to someone, apart from the signifiers (words) I pronounce, I use my face, my voice, my gaze, my body: this set of signifiers completes my signifying with a signification which is not present in any of the elements which make it up – only in the *Set* of them all. *Sets* possess qualities which their parts lack.

6 'Nunca eu tivera querido/ dizer palavra tão louca./ Bateu-me o vento na boca/ e depois no teu ouvido./ Levou somente a palavra/ deixou ficar o sentido./ O sentido está guardado/ no rosto com que te miro,/ neste perdido suspiro/ que te segue alucinado,/ no meu sorriso suspenso,/ como um beijo malogrado.' 'Canção', Cecília Meireles 1901–1964, Rio de Janeiro.

'I have never meant to speak so wild a word. The air strikes my mouth/ and then your ear./ I only sent the word/ and left behind its sense./ The sense is stored within my gaze,/ In the lost breath/ that follows you, hallucinated/ in the smile which hangs upon my face/ Like a failed kiss.'

7 The thick-soled, laced boot or buskin, reaching to knee or calf, worn by actors of ancient Greek and Roman tragedies. AJ

8 The polysemy of the word permits, in these modern times, the word *liberty*, for example, to be used to designate any restriction that is placed on the existence of others. *Liberalism* means the absence of any limits constraining the deployment of the economic power of the strong against the poor and destitute. *Democracy* means all the candidates in an election have the same right to buy time on the TV and space in the papers, if they have the money.

9 There is no English word for this French adjective, part of the lexicon of semiotics, referring to non-verbal sign-based communication. AJ

10 On encountering the Being in its unicity, the artist, the spectator, or the lover, comes face to face with the Infinite. The object of the love is always the Singular, the One; however all Unicity is a Set, as we observed earlier, wherein resides the Infinite, which is the impossible meeting in which each Unicity is a new Universe. The lover seeks the One – with the exception of the pathological Don Juan who loves no-one: he loves love, he loves loving; Narcissus, another clinical case, loves himself.

   Some forms of the psychological structures generically called *Madness* work in much the same way: for people in the grip of these conditions the *Sets* disintegrate and they lose themselves in the desperate perception of each one of the beings and things which make up the *Set*, without being capable of forming new *Sets*. There are sick people who see only the terrifying pores that make us penetrable and cannot see the skin which protects our bodies. Or they form entirely autonomous *Sets* which are referential neither to the real, nor to our collective perception.

11 In this search, he encounters the Singular, or the Single *way* of creating or discovering new *Sets* which only the Artist can perceive – in the fashion of the *madman* – but which we can all, by means of his art, derive pleasure from. And in this search we meet ourselves, like Fernando Pessoa: 'No-one loves another, unless they love that of themselves which is in, or presumed to be in, the other!' ('Ninguém a outro ama, se não que ama o que de si há nele, ou é suposto!')

12 In the same way that (as Vinicius de Moraes says) love is 'not immortal, . . . since it is only a flame . . . but shall be infinite while it lasts . . .'), the enjoyment of the work of art is not the same each time that we encounter it. We can discover it afresh each time or lose it for always.

13 Knowing that every Unicity is a new Set which comprehends Unicities that contain and are contained by Sets, full of Unicities, and so on, *ad Infinitum*.

14 The tree should not hide the forest, as the popular saying goes, but nor does the forest have the right to hide each tree that is lost within it – nor each shrub, each stem of flowers, each petal of each flower.

15 'O Aleijadinho' is the popular nickname (meaning 'the little cripple') given to architect and sculptor, Antônio Francisco Lisbôa, (1738–1814), the most famous Brazilian exponent of the

rococo style, who designed and decorated many eighteenth century churches and convents in the gold-rich Minas Gerais area. AJ

16 When, through Love or Art, we penetrate the unicity of a Being, we penetrate the Infinite. It would be foolish to imagine that the Infinite would only be infinite outwards and into the distance – . . . If it is true that there is or exists an Infinite, it cannot have limits *within*: the Infinite is not only infinite beyond the stars and the galaxies, but also within each atom of our body. The infinitely large is exactly the same as the infinitely small because it has no limits. The Infinite destroys concepts of large and small, far and close. All becomes very close because all is very far away, all is small because all is so large. We cannot understand or apprehend what Infinity is, like we cannot understand our own inevitable Death.

In each strand of my hair there are trillions of Milky Ways and Planetary Systems, sidereal objects attracted by voracious black holes. We should not fall into the same error as Parmenides (515BC – ?), the Greek philosopher who stated that the Universe was infinite in all directions and yet that it had a starting point and was likely to be spherical. Now, if it began at a particular point – here – and had a particular shape – the sphere – it would be finite, since form is the limit of Being and Not-Being, and, as we all know, Not-being *is not*. Isn't that so?

All unicity is multiple, in all senses and in all directions – that is *Infinite*. *Sets* conjoin *Unicities* but each *Unicity* is a *Set*: each atom (the indivisible) divides into protons, neutrons, electrons, etc. Each proton, each quark, each anti-quark, each penta-quark. The infinite is the vertigo of thought!

17 Empathy in Aristotle was intimately linked to *Anagnorisis* (the moment of recognition, which coincided with the Protagonist's discovery of the Truth), when the Protagonist explained the reasons for his actions and admitted his errors, so as to convince the audience to do the same – emotion was always linked to reason. No sacrifices were in vain.

Anagnorisis is a particular rational and ethical moment of the Tragedy, but Empathy should also contain the same combination of Reason-Action-Emotion that should prevail throughout the play.

The Chorus, in Greek Tragedy, frequently, but not always, incorporated and even verbally explained Virtue, Knowledge, Wisdom, and expressed a solid moral support for the actions the Protagonist should take or should have taken. Hollywood films, on the contrary, use pure emotional empathy to brutalise their spectators.

The modern equivalent of the Greek Chorus is, on TV, the anonymous mass of fans in the auditorium of live shows, who are able only frantically to scream their adoration at the stars on stage.

I would even go as far as to say that this is the most dangerous combination of Empathy (reduced to mere violence) and Anagnorisis (reduced to shrill shrieks).

18 Francis Fukuyama, *The End of History*, 1992.

19 Algebraic equation consisting of two terms. AJ

20 Notorious massacre in a US school in April 1999 in which two students killed twelve of their fellow students and a teacher before committing suicide.

21 In November 2004, it was reported that the United States had launched a new video-game in which the user takes Lee Harvey Oswald's place and shoots at John Kennedy's car as it passes: when you hit the target, blood spurts over the virtual asphalt.

22 The Portuguese word *translação* is any kind of transposition: it can be translated as 'metaphor', or 'transfer', which of course goes back to the Greek etymology of the word, from *meta*, implying 'a change' and *pherein* meaning 'to bear'. AJ

23 The evolution of the hominids who metamorphosed into today's Human Being was not a single unbroken straight line. In the Isle of Flores, Indonesia (cf. *Nature*, September 2004) they discovered the skeleton of a hominid dating from the period when Neanderthal men and women mysteriously disappeared, twenty or thirty thousand years ago, just after they coincided on Earth with Cro-Magnon and perhaps other still undiscovered species. The Human Being may be the result of crossings of Neanderthals, Cro-Magnons, Homo Floresienses and yet others, still buried in the ground.

24 Metaphors are to be found in at least three grammatical forms: the Adjectival Metaphor: 'Capitalism is a paper tiger!'; the Adverbial Metaphor: 'The car flew down the track' (where the verb 'to fly' is used adverbially, to describe a way of running, and where the verb 'to run', which is modified, is eclipsed); and the Substantive Metaphor, which is any work of art which trans-substantiates reality. There are also metaphors by Metonymy: 'Drinking a glass of wine'.

25 Italian in original. A proverb, which loosely translates as 'Even if it's not true, it makes a good story'. AJ

26 The extreme delicacy and complexity of the cells called neurons obliges Nature to make a curious exception: apart from the skull, all the bones of our body are inside it and help support it: in the head however, the bone structure envelopes the brain and gives it protection. There must be something pretty important in there.

27 A mass in church, for example, apart from the sense of sight, stimulates the ear, with its ambient music, the palate and the nose, with its sweetmeats, and the tactile with its dances.

28 The *signal* is a sensory stimulus (sound, image, etc.) either agreed between people, or automatically inferred, which carries a particular, limited meaning: *this* means *that*! It is a warning. Whereas the *symbol*, though also settled by convention, has no limits. Green on the traffic light is the *signal* which allows you to go, but the colour green is a *symbol* of hope. You could say that a fallen tree on the street was a *signal* of heavy winds, while the same felled tree painted on a triangle at the roadside, is a *symbol* of danger, though it is a *sign* for the traffic. The *signal* can also have acquired its significance by memory: a black cloud is a *signal* of rain. As for the *sign*, it can have magic powers attributed to it, as in those of the Horoscope, or mnemonic signs, like those in heraldry. *Insignia*, which reveal status, can be made up of signals, symbols and signs.

29 Jean-Bédel Bokassa (1921–1996), president of the Central African Republic, 1966–1979.

30 Some spectacles, given their cathartic nature, turn into orgiastic rituals – like, for example, those huge musical gatherings where no-one goes just to hear the music, but for symbolic – or not so symbolic – orgies. The distance the Beatles kept from their audiences, an apparent disdain, like frigid lovers, exacerbated still further their fans' desperate quest for paroxysm.

31 There is, apparently, an expression, *o boi do piranha*, the piranha's cow, which refers to the fact that when a farmer has to drive his herd across a river, he sends one cow ahead first, to see if it is safe – if it is unlucky, it will be the piranha's cow . . . AJ

32 The motor neurons which allow us to move our big toe, are easily the simplest. Lula, having lost the little finger of his left hand, went on to be elected president of Brazil, and is doing fine; Roosevelt lost the motor capacity of his legs, but continued to lead his country. But, if either of them had lost a piece of their brain, the world would have been on the verge of catastrophe, as in fact it is.

33 It is a running joke in Brazil (as in many other countries) that no-one knows the second verse of the National Anthem. AJ

34 When the CTO began its activities in Rio in 1986, in poor communities, there were few NGOs that applied themselves to such tasks: today, many are dedicated to delivering artistic programmes similar to those that already exist for the middle class, preparing actors and dancers for TV, theatre and the cinema. Reports in the media about exceptionally talented youngsters are common, people who have been discovered in the *favelas* who are going to have a career in soap operas, or dancers selected to continue their studies in New York and even at the Moscow Bolshoi ballet. This has happened, and it is great that it happens – however, it is not our function, not does it form part of our objectives.

This application, in poor communities, of the same programmes and methods as used by the middle and upper classes, brings in its wake the same competitive ideology and the same eulogising of the *most capable*, the *exceptional*: the ideology of *first place*, of *the winner*. To stimulate this competition, some organisations even bring TV stars to perform with children from the *favela*. This, of course, is not our aim.

Our function, by contrast, is to prepare the participants in our groups to be Multipliers of Art, following our maxim that '*You only learn when you teach*', our objective being to reach the whole fabric of society and not only to reveal exceptional hidden talents.

35 As defined in the *Aurelio Dictionary* (Brazilian equivalent of the *Oxford English Dictionary*).

36 Julian Boal, in his exercise *The Dance of Work*, cites researchers who show that movements made as part of work were, in many cases, the origin of dances known worldwide, such as the tap dance, which comes from the sound of the steps of North American slaves, when they went around the houses of their masters, wearing wooden shoes with noisy iron toe-caps, so that their masters would know where they were at all times; or the graceful circular movements of the hands of Andalusian dancers performing flamenco, which originated in the movements of fruit-pickers; or the curved movements of the Capoeira dancers-fighters, which derive from sugar cane cutting.

37 See *The Legislative Theatre*, Augusto Boal, Routledge, 1998.

38 Nature does not make a leap.

39 *Literatura de cordel* (string literature) are pamphlets or booklets that hang from a piece of string (cordel) in the places where they are sold. These are long, narrative poems with woodcut illustrations on the cover, often done by the poet. The largest concentration of this type of popular literature is in North-Eastern Brazil. AJ

THEATRE AS A MARTIAL ART

The idea of the globalisation of economy and culture, which today is proffered as modern, is in fact older than the hills. What is modern about it is the use of computers, the speed of the Stock Exchange and the vertiginous global movement of capital which results.

Every day the stock exchanges move a trillion and a half dollars around the world, and barely 1 per cent of this money contributes to the creation of wealth: according to *Le Monde Diplomatique*, 99 per cent of it consists of speculative transactions in search of profit. This astronomical quantity is as modern as the payment of interest on external debt – un-audited debts, even if they were incurred by dictators who, of course, kept the bulk of the money in their own pockets.

International economic relations, though played out in the fantasy of the discreet elegance of diplomacy, have always been of a predatory nature, since they are a product of a predatory animal, the human being. Whenever a nation, tribe or empire achieves hegemonic power over its neighbours, it always seeks to undermine them. Never do the strong extend to the weak the hand of friendship.

Hitler's *Thousand Year Reich* did not hesitate to apply 'final solution' to those who were different. The *Pax Romana* was nothing less than the globalisation of Caesar's power. Attila, the scourge of God, invaded lands and wherever his horse trod the grass would never grow again. Let it not be said that globalising is modern: human voracity has always been with us and today it is at the peak of its form.

The diaphanous mantle of hypocrisy hides the naked cannibalism of globalisation. When Iraq was invaded for having occupied Kuwait – an event which doubled the price of a barrel of oil – the sacred duty of Humanitarian Intervention was invoked. Saddam was bombed and the price of a barrel fell. This same humanitarian duty to intervene is forgotten in Sierra Leone, where the amputation of the arms and legs of political prisoners, even children, is routine; likewise in Rwanda and in Eritrea, where tractors bulldoze putrefying cadavers into open graves, piled high.

Bill Clinton has a seductive smile. On a visit to Vietnam, he exhorted the Vietnamese leaders to pay more attention to human rights – and who would argue with that? This is a minor detail: Clinton was president of the nation which twenty-five years ago dropped tons of napalm on Vietnam and killed two million Vietnamese – where was their respect for human rights? Two million hypocrisies!

I would be in favour of total globalisation if its objective was the promotion of health, education and science. But what has been globalised instead is the search for profits.

According to King Alfonso VI of Spain: 'If God had asked my opinion before he created the world, I would have recommended something simpler, a less complicated human being, without such arrogance and greed'. Me too.

We are not to blame for the way the world is or the way it has been in the past, but we will be responsible for what it becomes in the future.

I want to make a startling Revelation: Life feeds on Death. Nature is merciless, cruel, amoral. In nature, the fat eat the thin, the strong engulf the weak. For us to live, we have to kill, whether it be a lettuce leaf or a three hundred kilo pig: this is our animal nature, which we carry into our human relations.

The human being has still not humanised itself and lives dangling by its tail, leaping from branch to branch; still it does not allow itself to be guided by morality. We live pre-Neanderthal times and, just because we have learnt to knot our tie, we think that we are already *Homo sapiens* and, worse (what pretension!) *Sapiens sapiens*!

We should face up to the truth staring us in the face: we are beasts! Let's get that into our heads! Man is the wolf of man – as the poet has it. To which I add, in prose: man eats . . . and is edible!

In this world of rancour and hate, shocks and jolts, Goodness is a human invention – it is not born spontaneously like a flower of the field. It has to be taught and learnt, but the human being is a bad teacher and a worse pupil.

This is our huge task: to shake off our savage nature and create a culture where goodness is possible and solidarity sought after.

This is a job for culture. Culture, however, is not limited to the works exhibited in our museums, or the shows we pay to get into. Culture is how we do things, what we do, for whom and by whom we do them.

We have to assume our human condition of creator. We are not beavers who build their dams without knowing what they are doing, because they are genetically programmed to do so, or birds who always make the same nest, and sing the same song without choosing the score. We are not *Uirapurus*, who bring forest life to a halt with the beauty of their sound, when they open their beaks to sing. We are capable of singing and building, capable of inventing song and architecture! The *Uirapuru* knows how to sing but does not know that it is singing – whereas we, even if we are singing out of tune, know that we are singing out of tune.

Art is part of Culture because culture is the human being. It is the very part of the being which makes it human. It is what distinguishes us from the animal. To make culture, to invent, the artist has to be free, to do what he or she wants. If he submits to the market, if he accepts its laws and ceases to be a creator, he ceases to be an artist.

I admire those business people who make an art of their business, and I pity those artists who make a business of their art.

In the globalising world, culture and art, because they are so powerful, are stolen from us and end up serving the same purpose as commerce, i.e. profit. When we go to a Hollywood film, it is not only the plot we have to swallow. It is the Texan hats, the bad whisky, the music; the *Hello Joe! Go to hell, Jack!*; the cars exploding on hi-tech steel bridges and tossed into a sea riddled with jet-skis, the police sirens, the violence, the latest model of machine gun (which will be immediately adopted by the our narco-traffickers, who always keep up with the latest martial technology).

A film will sell more merchandise than the explicit commercial advertisements. The mere fact that the majority of the films on cable TV have an English soundtrack already makes us think in English, even those who do not know the meaning of the words.

This is the only reason why, in the *favelas* of Rio, one can come across people who answer to the name of Shirley Temple de Oliveira, Clark Gable da Silva, John Wayne dos Santos – though, thank God, we have yet to encounter Sylvester Stallone de Deus, Michael Jackson da Encarnação or Madonna Mia do Encantado.

The dangers of empathy: the mere fact of watching on the television so-called 'situation comedies' (lacking as they are in the slightest wit) or 'romances' (as loveless as they are), makes us assimilate the feelings and behaviours of the characters, even when we know them to be dull. We sit there, witless and stupefied. TV has become a criminal form of hypnotism.

The globalisation of profit imposes the homogenisation of human beings: all must be the same and consume the same, dress the same way and eat the same burgers (fresh from the mad cow). Globalisation imposes norms of behaviour, values, ideology and aesthetic taste.

When France demanded *l'exception culturelle* – i.e. that the cinema and other arts should be exempted from the GATT trade agreements – it was not the intrinsic value of its works of art that it was protecting. It was guarding against the danger that the worm of North American culture would take up residence in its belly.

The screens of the cinema are shop windows of Merchandise and Morality – the Merchandise sells itself to us, and the Morality inflicts itself on us.

It is important for the globalisers to destroy national cultures, local cultures, where they are trying to export their business; it is important for these elements of national identity to be decimated, since culture is identity and the globalisers need to destroy identities to sell their products better.

Whenever we listen to Brazilian music, whether Bossa Nova or traditional samba, we see our face, even if it is ugly. Watching our films, even our soap-operas, we say: 'That's us!' – even though we may not like it. Today, we are banned from seeing ourselves in our art. We have to listen to rock and *heavy metal*, to see *Godzillas* and *Spidermen*! Globalisation inflicts on all of us the same language, in which we must say: 'Yes sir!'[1]

This is the curious paradox of globalisation: to globalise it is necessary to abolish dialogue, to isolate the individual – not in order to strengthen his individuality, but so that the very differences which make him unique may disappear.

In art, the artist, creator of the new, is eliminated; enter the technical artisan – the one who reproduces the same model,[2] *ad infinitum*. We see always the same movie.

Globalisation is the death of the artist!

Today, it is almost impossible to be an artist and survive in the cultural market – few manage it. If we want to help to change the world with our art – to change our country, our state, our street – it is imperative to work where art is not bought and sold, where art is alive, where we are all artists – in the places where the people live: in the streets, the *favelas*, the encampments of the MST, in the unions, in the churches. That is where we find those who need their own identity in order to liberate themselves from oppression, even when they are *dominated by the dominant ideas*, even when they are alienated. We must have hopes, but no illusions.

* * *

There exist today two fundamental ideologies in this terminal world: one says that Humanity is a single entity, that we are brothers, and the State must offer equal opportunities to all, without regard to birth, bank card or cheque book.

The other humanity can be explained by an old story, the Raft of Medusa, which tells the history of group of shipwrecked castaways adrift at sea. Having no food, first they decide to chop up and eat the dead, then the sick, followed later by the defenceless little children. Wanting to save themselves, they go on eating each other till only one survivor remains on the raft.

Dying of hunger, the single survivor starts to eat himself, beginning with the parts of his body most easily dispensed with: the fingers and the left arm, and the leg on the same side. He goes on eating his own body and ends up consuming his intestines, having found nothing more nutritious, including head and heart – both useless organs! The last thing that the castaway eats is his own tongue and his mouth! After that he eats nothing more . . . he spits out a tooth!

As yet, the rich in Brazil are eating only street children, landless workers, blacks and unemployed people . . . but the day will come when they will eat themselves!

This cannibal ideology is also called Modernity. Cannibalism is modern! They say that left and right no longer exist, that these are things of the French Revolution. So I will not talk of left and right, out of fashion as these words are. I will speak of Humanism and Cannibalism – enough hypocrisy!

In this contest of Humanism versus Cannibalism – all over the world the cannibals are still winning!

In a world trying to robotise itself, the work of art loses its *raison d'être* and gives way to the single de-personalised product: the Market grafts on to us a Prosthesis of Desire – it extirpates our own desire and implants in us the desire of the Market.

I am not against the market that satisfies our needs: I am against the market that creates in us artificial needs to buy their products.

So that more is bought and sold, I have to sing with the throat of the hit singer; to dance with another dancer's legs, rather than the legs I was born with; to see the world with others' eyes – rather than my own; to cry the tear that is not mine, to smile the smile they chisel onto my face, like stone sculpted.

All I ask is: let us sing with our own voice, even if it is hoarse, let us dance with our own body, even if it is doddery; let us speak our own speech, even if we are uncertain.

This must be the art of the Humanist, the one who says no to Robotisation, who affirms differences, and out of those differences, unity: we are men and women, we have black skin and white skin, our eyes are blue and brown, and our hope is green!

We are different – as a result of the cultures we grow up in and the lands we live in. And we are the same – in our determination to be ourselves, in our unwillingness to become extensions of the great God Market.

Globalisation craves monologue: to combat globalisation, we need dialogue, in unions and in churches, in schools and in political parties, in the sciences and in the arts, in the solitude of the psychoanalyst's couch and in the multitudinous gatherings of theatre in the street.

The theatre is a privileged means by which we may find out who we are, in the creation of images of our desire – we are our desire, or we are nothing.

Why theatre? Because there are arts, like music, which organise sound and silence in time; and others, like painting, which organise form and colour in space; and then there are arts like the theatre, which organise human actions in space and time.

In the act of organising human actions, they show where we have been, where we are, and where we are going; who we are, what we feel and what we desire. For this reason we must all do theatre, to discover who we are and find out who we could become.

In the Theatre of the Oppressed, the people who come on stage to recount an episode of their lives are simultaneously narrator and narrated – for this reason, they are able to imagine themselves in the future.

People go on stage to do theatre, because theatre cannot be done alone and in order to all say 'I', before coming together in another beautiful word: 'we'!

The theatre is a mirror in which we can see our vices and our virtues, according to Shakespeare. And it can also be transformed into a magic mirror, as in the Theatre of the Oppressed, a mirror we can enter if we do not like the image it shows us and, by penetrating it, rehearse modifications of this image, rendering it more to our liking. In this mirror we see the present, but can invent the future of our dreams: the act of transforming is in itself transformatory. In the act of changing our image, we are changing ourselves, and by changing ourselves in turn we change the world.

Theatre is both art and weapon. Today, more than ever, struggling for our cultural survival, the theatre is an *art* which reveals our identity and a *weapon* which preserves it.

To resist, it is not enough to say no. It is necessary to desire! It is necessary to dream. Not the technicolour dream of television which takes the place of the black and white of harsh reality, but the dream which lays the ground for a new reality, a new reality where the quest is to *unify* Humanity, but not to make human beings *uniform*. Today, theatre is a martial art!

THE INSUBMISSIVE PROTAGONIST

Few contemporaneous texts survive on the beginnings of the theatre in Greece, the tradition in which we follow. Having only little documentary evidence, fragmented accounts, we are obliged to imagine these beginnings: we are condemned to Imagination!

In Ancient Greece – like everywhere else – after arduous collective labour, men liked to celebrate, at Liberty, the end of Discipline. Discipline and Liberty, inseparable twins, always at each other's throats!

For any team-based activity to be possible, Discipline is indispensable. In house-building, the painter cannot paint before the walls are erected; the roof concludes the elevation work, after the foundations, never the other way round. In all construction, discipline is obligatory.

When the work is done, this discipline no longer applies. In the topping-out celebration, the builders knock back the beer, and sing and dance to their hearts' content. The tongue is off the leash. Everyone gets to stretch their limbs. Licence rules and runs off at the mouth. Censorship sleeps, till the shutters come back down. Discipline is broken. Its mission is accomplished, and now it's the turn of Liberty.

That is how it was in Greece, at harvest-time. The farmers worked the land, in a disciplined fashion, from sunrise to sunset, for weeks and months; then came the harvest of the grape and then came the wine. It was normal for them to get drunk and sing and dance in homage to Dionysus, God of joy, God of boozing. Alcohol was fundamental, not accidental; alcohol was the touch-paper of liberty.

The dances and songs of the Greek tillers of the land when their harvest was done, were as spontaneous as those of the builder of today, on finishing the house. They came from the soul. Creative anarchy. Which could, however, be destructive.

This liberty needed to be contained within parameters. Limits needed to be imposed, but could liberty in chains still be liberty? The Aristocracy thought so – it could not allow this delirium. If heretofore work had been the subject of discipline, now liberty too had to be taken care of. It was too dangerous! It could, *in extremis*, result in the destruction of what had been constructed.

A necessary contradiction: the tension between freedom and order. Free, the body invented dance, the dance it carried within; free, the body cut its own caper in space and time! Choreography intervened, traced the movement made, explained the gesture, marked the rhythm, limited the space. Along came the poet and wrote his verses: no more free thought, no more creative chaos: enter stage right, premeditated Order.

Poetry and choreography were advances. But liberty ended there – here lies liberty. Something more solemn than the explosions of Bacchus was inaugurated; the Dithyrambic Song.

This song is the shout imprisoned, uproar with rhyme and rhythm, sanctioned implosion. Wildness civilised. Joy by stopwatch, carefully dosed. And the show, the spectacle – there was no such thing till then – came into being with everyone dancing the *same* dance, singing the *same* religious song. The Aristocracy, its fear lost, applauded: now, for sure, it knew what it was going to see; the authorised version.

Thespis was a *polyvalent* man: poet, choreographer, actor and . . . drunk.[3] He wrote poems and, lost in the mass of the Chorus, sung for all he was worth. He devised movements and executed them in the dithyrambic procession, in collective harmony. The obedient artist, listening to, and obeying, himself.

One day, there came to see his show the great Solon, the legislator who had just revoked the Draconian Code; to this very day, Draco still inspires fear with that famous *tooth for a tooth*, which became Biblical, and *eye for an eye*, with its threat of perpetual night.

Solon lived long, he was the Legislator who promulgated democratic legislation. Just to give you a sense of the man, let me say that, amongst other things, Solon had the brilliant idea that all citizens should be pardoned for all their debts, as in the blessed Biblical Jubilee which proposed the same every fifty years. Is this not a brilliant idea by the author of the book of Leviticas?! Everything is zero-ed and no-one would have to owe anything to anyone, marvellous! Debtors all loved it! Creditors were not so keen!

Solon pardoned all debts incurred up to then, but he did not abolish the unjust distribution of land, the Greek *latifundia* (landed estates), cause of new and even greater debts. Every worker without land was obliged to hand over to his landowner four-fifths of his harvest. No-one today could keep up with this, nor could they then. Result: anyone who was part of this body of landless rural workers had no option but to sign more papers, incurring more debts.

Solon did everything by halves. He did not put an end to prostitution, but he was the first public man to create *tolerance zones* for 'working women'. The greater part of Greece became one big wild *zone*!

Solon, the All-Powerful, came to see the Thespian show! With Solon, in the audience it was like having Zeus in the house. Zeus help us! There were tremors of happiness and fear! Will he like it? Will he like me?! Solon, leaning on a cane made from the tusk of a Libyan elephant (he was lame) seated himself in the front row.

Dithyrambs were religious processions, ambulatory in nature, but then as now, there would be a place reserved for the authorities, a sort of *Praça da Apoteose* (Apotheosis Square),[4] where the members of the chorus put forth with even greater religious ardour. Solon, the head of government had his own private box there.

The show started off, with all decorum. In the middle of the poem, dancing frenetically, spurred on by courage and by fear, Thespis could not contain himself. He felt a strange thing, an itch in his throat and he called to everyone in earshot: 'Hold me back, I'm going to lose it.'

No-one did hold him back as they were benumbed with fear. Thespis, crazed, bounded away from the chorus and . . . answered back to it. Something came over him. He 'lost it', as he had so graciously put it, and he began to say whatever came into his head! He was possessed, like the priest of Bacchus, as if he was in the midst of the Mystery of Eleusis[5] and had taken several doses of whatever they took (– to this very day, we know not what. Maybe Mexican hallucinogenic mushrooms or what the Saint Daime cult use from the Amazon, who knows? Whatever it was, it provoked a mild delirium tremens . . .). Thespis spoke of the city, of politics, of religion, of men and of laws . . . delirium.

This thing which, at first, appeared to be nothing more than an undisciplined actor's off-the-cuff one-liner, an irresponsible gag, turned into well-articulated discourse – dangerous.

Shock! Horror! Fear! A mere member of the chorus had dared to answer back. Worse yet, he had done it in front of the Head of State! The fact that he had done it proved that it was possible to do! Before now, no-one had thought of this . . . Everyone went along obediently, singing in chorus . . . and freedom was possible . . . but no-one knew. Freedom IS possible!

Thespis went on answering back. The man was possessed! The Chorus sang poetry, he replied in prose. The chorus sang the virtues of the prevailing Morality, the Official Religion – he proclaimed his profane ideas, adorned with his own words, chosen on the spur of the moment, as his fancy took him.

And what a fancy it was!

Great puzzlement: what on earth was this!? In the Chorus, everyone sang and danced in chorus, as befitted them! How could it be possible for one man – however great a fellow Thespis thought he was – to leap out of the rigid choreographic formation and challenge it, uttering a provocative *No* to the obligatory and customary *Yes*!?!

Solon was silent, like someone who did not want a quarrel, pretending that he was not aware of what was happening in front of his eyes, that he had not heard right, making out that he was half deaf, and he just sat there, but rage cried out in his spleen. After the show, he limped off to the dressing rooms, to visit the *artistes*, to offer them his heartfelt congratulations – after all, he was a popular legislator. He had to go through the motions! He spoke with everyone, with each member of the chorus. He shared recollections from his life, praised the gods and played the true gent.

Stopping to talk to Thespis, in a hollow voice quarried out of hatred, he asked him, quietly, almost biting the man's ear in his incandescent rage: 'Do you not feel shamefaced to lie like this, quite consciously, in front of so many people? There was the Chorus doing splendidly, patiently speaking the truth, in tune. And along you come, shameless as you like, and start spouting lies!'

Thespis protested that he had not been lying: he had spoken the truth of his *character* which, clearly, was not him – for himself, his thinking was totally in tune with Solon's, why, of course.

Without knowing it, Thespis had created a character who was not the Chorus; the Protagonist, *Protos*, the first, the person who is alone, who rebels, who thinks and acts for himself – without *mimeses*, without mimetism, without imitating anyone! – discovering who he is, opening up paths, showing the possible, becoming the figure that penetrates the thickets of the unknown. Wandering fearlessly and accepting the consequences – of which there are always some, and punishment is always prompt!

Thespis, face to face with Solon, alarmed at what he saw, elaborated a theory: 'I do not feel any shame, Lord Solon, because I did not lie! What your Lordship saw was not the reality that your Lordship and I inhabit and live: it was a theatrical play!'

He used the word 'play' in the sense of performance – like we in Brazil say *representação* (representation), or *jogo*, or the French say *jeu*, both the latter meaning 'acting' as well as 'game'. In truth, it means: theatre, fiction, possibility, image or, who knows, *representation of the real, rather than the mere reproduction of it*. As Thespis had not read the theory of the Theatre of the Oppressed, he did not know that *the image of the real is real as an image*. Solon, who had never read my book either, died without knowing that he had gone to the very heart of the truth. Here he spoke a truth, out of pure intuition:

'Be that as it may, this play of yours is very dangerous! The people may not understand that it is just a little play, they may even think that your ideas are a good idea, and allow themselves to be influenced by your nefarious suggestions . . . It would not take much, if I didn't speak out, for this play of yours, this little game, this lie, to contaminate our customs, to become truth . . . Which is not good. So let it be known that, henceforward, it is only right for the Chorus to sing, and the Chorus can only sing words and phrases which have been written down and then read by us, before being sung by you. These libertarian inventions are most dangerous! Too much creativity for my taste.'

To strike awe in Thespis, he gave an example of atrocious punishment:

'Look what happened to Prometheus: he was a demi-god, a nice guy, who went astray – he gave mankind fire, he betrayed his peers, and that is dangerous! Fire burns. Prometheus gave mankind a bad example: he showed that what belongs to the gods can also be used by men. The fire was *play*, a bit of fun – but it burnt for real! Prometheus ended up tied to a rock, with his liver being devoured by eagles. Why? Because when it is fire today, it is power tomorrow, and the day after that who knows what? Men are greedy, they always want more . . .'

He concluded, threateningly:

'The same thing goes for you: the actual words you used do not matter – what matters is that you said that it is possible to say such things! Do you understand me? You spoke to the effect that it is possible to speak. You showed these people that every individual has the capacity to think with his own mind without asking me what I think, that anyone can choose their own words, without repeating mine! That is bad! A very bad example to set!

I know it is the case, of course, you spoke the truth, but I do not want anyone to know it!'

Before he went off, he growled: 'Don't do this any more, got it? I don't like it . . . don't like it one little bit . . . No, no, no!' And with this lapidary phrase the Western theatre almost failed to be invented.

Obstinate Thespis, stubborn even when he was on the ropes, wanted to continue being the *Protagonist*. It is very nice to be a Protagonist and he wanted to continue *protagonising* his life, even while the chorus members continued their work of chorusing the words, singing in tune, as one, words they did not even understand. It is difficult to go back to a supporting role once you have been a protagonist. No-one likes it; everyone likes to step out on to the pitch – or onto the stage.

The audience at this memorable opening – with the exception of the sour-faced big-shots (there are always some!) – adored the idea, adored this rebirth of liberty, and wanted more. To improvise is to live! Life is an eternal improvisation, or it is no life at all!

Impasse. What now? Thespis thought that it wasn't good to give the impression of lying, and he did not want to lie in being obliged to say that he was lying: it would be lying to say that he was lying! It was not true that he was lying. He was speaking the truth – his truth, which was one of the possible truths. That's dialectics.

The Chorus was anxious: 'What's happening?' they asked. 'What do we do now?' No-one knew what to do. 'Can we or can't we? To cut or not to cut? We want to carry on like you were doing – we sing, you respond – but the Boss doesn't seem keen on the innovations . . . he looked daggers at us, out of the corner of his eye.'

Where was the truth and where were the lies? Thespis's truth denied the truth of the Chorus which, in turn, denied liberty. If anyone was lying, it was not he, since he was only affirming a contradictory truth. So what now?

In order that no-one would have to lie and, at the same time, all might be able to speak their own truths, Thespis, creative man that he was, had yet another, even more fantastic idea: he invented the Mask, which allowed him to say: 'This, which looks like me, is not me, it is another: I am me, I am an actor, and he is the Character!'

He invented the Costumes for the Protagonist, while the chorus members continued to dress in vine leaves, like a uniform, like a school of fantasy Samba: 'I don't dress like that, the Character does, that's how he dresses!' And he shod himself in *kothornoi*, shoes with bulky high heels: 'I am a little guy, but the Protagonist is tall – look, you can see for yourself, he is not me, he is someone else – he is enormous.'

Once *characterised*, the Character was not Thespis: he was the Other.[6] Actor and Character – one flesh hitherto – were now divorced and became two, the Actor and the Mask. Thespis could continue being himself, disguised in the other, behind the Costume, on top of the *kothornoi* and behind the Mask.

To this very day, in the groups of ordinary participants in Carnival known as *blocos sujos*,[7] no-one goes out in the street with his own face, as he is, just clad in jacket and tie or whatever. People paint their faces bright colours, men disguise themselves as women, and women as Eve in high heels!

Because the Actor *was* the Character without *being* him, the art of the actor became known in Greece as the art of the *hypocrite* – that is, the person who pretends to be a person he is not. He pretends to be, but how? Pretends to be by being – because clearly he *was* (in the sense of being, existing); if he *were not*, he couldn't *be* (the Character). In Physics, two things cannot occupy the same place in the space but in theatre (as well as in life) many characters and many persons can occupy the same actor in a play, and the same individual in life. The actor is the character and he is also himself – not half and half, totally both of them.

Even though it might have been only a seeming, that seeming *was*, that seeming really *existed*! In the art of the actor, two beings existed: the Actor – hidden behind the mask – and the mask itself. The art of the actor, because of this, was named thus: *Hypocrisy* (*Hypokrisis* – putting on a mask).

Please, tell no-one, but herewith may it stand proven that the theatre and hypocrisy were born from the same womb, on the same day. Ever since, this division of the one being into two, this dichotomy, Actor and Character, has been and remains one of the most fascinating themes of the theatre, and of psychology.

Thespis established his creation, but was obliged to give way on one major point. In the following season, he went to find his *Maecenas*,[8] protector of the arts, the *Archon Eponymous*,[9] one of the three Legislators who previously ran things in the city as a triumvirate – before Solon resolved to order things alone; the *Archon Eponymous* was the one who dealt with the theatrical festivals.

Then as now, theatre shows cost a lot; someone has to pay the production costs. At that time, there were people like *Maecenas*, who nowadays call themselves 'angels' (on Broadway) or the Ministry of Culture (in France) – as we see, the Maecenases of this world go back a long way. Thespis's backer was a kind-hearted millionaire, who was soon saying:

> 'My dear Thespis, I understand. You are a true artist, creator, a genius – you will find a
> place in History, I am almost sure. You will be talked about for months, for years
> to come. The idea of inventing the Protagonist, the one who speaks what he wants,

who says whatever comes into his head – that is a marvellous idea. My sincere congratulations!'

Thespis was happy, but his Maecenas had not finished speaking, worse was to come:

'It so happens that I am not an artist. I am a producer of tragedy, you follow. My name is linked to yours. What you say on stage, it is as if I were saying it. So look here, dear Thespis: I cannot spend my money on plays whose content I only find out on the day of the show. I am not censoring you, I swear I am not, perish the thought, we live in a true democracy – *demos*, people, *kratia*, power or rule! In a democracy such as ours, every artist must be free, but – oh yes, there is a "but" in this story – his freedom has limits: it finishes when I have to start dipping in to the bank: if I am going to waste my money, I need to know what I am going to waste it on! It's right and proper that you should say what you want, but it's also right and proper that I should only pay for things that give me pleasure.'

Thespis was open-mouthed at the astonishing and unexpected lucidity of Lord Maecenas, who went on, warming to his theme:

'Cutting to the chase: if you want to continue receiving my little subsidies, you have to show me the text of your improvisation, put everything in writing on good quality papyrus, in triplicate with nice lettering, *before* beginning the rehearsals – because I do not like disagreeable surprises, OK? I want to read, in advance, all the Chorus's verses and every improvised speech made by your Protagonist!'

Improvisations cannot be censored – or they cease to be instantaneous creation. Like life in all its forms, to live is the art of improvising. When censored, improvisations become crystallised objects. Of course, actors have other languages that go with the words – their body, their body in space, their voices – and with these languages, they can of course say the opposite of what the words usually mean – but the words are still there.

The Greek theatre (let the historians say what they want!) was censored theatre: both by the Maecenases who financed only the shows that suited them, and by the priests of Dionysus. To this very day you can go to the theatre of the Athenian Acropolis and see the solitary marble armchair of the priest of Dionysus in all its overbearing glory! The censor was sitting in the front row!

Years later the aristocratic Aeschylus invented the *Deuteragonist*. Now there were two *Protagonists*, the one able to confirm or contradict the other. Aeschylus invented Dialogue. Sophocles, another nobleman, invented the *Tritagonist*! Tragic poets now had three actors at their disposal, three *Hypocrites*, wearing Masks: the number of characters could be greater, each actor playing more than one, since by changing their Mask and shading their voice they would not be recognised.

Hypocrisy was complete, once and for all: the separation between Actor and Character, the impossible divorce. Thespis was two-fold, like every good actor. Complex Hypocrisy: the actor pretended to be who he was not and was who he pretended to be!

> 'The poet is a feigner:
>
> So completely does he feign
>
> That the pain he truly feels
>
> He even feigns as pain'

Wrote Fernando Pessoa.[10]

So things went further, as the theatre slid once again on the toboggan of Liberty: the Chorus continued to sing the Official History but, with the invention of Dialogue, ideas could be counter-posed against other ideas, and nothing could guarantee that the ideas supported by those in Power would emerge as sovereign.

Dialogue is always dangerous because it creates *discontinuity* between one thought and another, between two opinions, feelings, possibilities; between them lodges the infinite, where all opinions are possible, all thoughts permitted. When, rather than the one and only Absolute Thought, two exist, creation is possible! Dialogue is democracy!

At the mere thought of this, a panic-stricken Plato vociferated: 'Look here, pay attention: in my *Republic*, theatre does not even make an entrance! Get out of here! Don't even think of it! That's all we need, for God's sake! Theatre – what a plague, what an awful thing! Get out of here!'

He shouted in the streets, from door to door: 'This world in which we live is corrupted!', with good reason, as if talking about our world today:

'It is the corruption of the ideal world, which *is* but does not *exist*, which is perfect, divine, marvellous: the World of Ideas! We are a pale imitation, a wretched shadow of what we should have been. The theatre is even worse! It is a shadow of that shadow, a pale imitation of a pale imitation, a corruption of a corruption! Down with the theatre!'

Mankind was damned even. Aristotle, by contrast, cocked his head, smiling, content to contradict the master: '*Amicus Plato . . . sed magis amica Veritas!*' he said – he spoke of course in good ancient Greek (which was modern, in his time), but it comes down to us in Latin, a language Aristotle never mastered, I guarantee you.

Translated into English, Aristotle said that he was a friend of Plato: '*Amicus Plato*'. He was however – '*magis amica Veritas*' – a greater friend of truth.

Aristotle explained: 'Things are not exactly as Plato goes around saying they are; he doesn't understand these matters very well. As far as I am concerned, the protagonist can wander at will and the spectators may even delight in his wanderings, taking pleasure in the same pleasure . . .', and he used the word *Empatia*, meaning that the spectators became so identified with the *Protagonist* that they would interrupt their own thoughts for a moment and think with the *Protagonist*'s mind, anaesthetising their own emotions and allowing themselves to be moved by the Protagonist's emotions. In other words: at this moment, there comes into being the *Prosthesis of Desire*.[11] The Protagonist, having divorced the Actor, now weds the subjugated Spectator, or rather weds the Prosthesis of Desire installed within him.

Aristotle went on: 'Even then, the enjoyment of the prohibited does not have the slightest importance because, as Thespis put it so well, "this is play, it is *representation*".'

The Platonic fellow travellers did not agree: 'I understand but, even so, it stands to reason . . . the person who enjoys something in a *representation* is going to want to enjoy it in reality . . . But he cannot enjoy what is forbidden.'

'That's where you and Plato are mistaken, flat wrong, OK! Stop worrying about the audience enjoying the protagonist's flaw, getting off on the sinning aplenty that takes place in the fiction: it is quite sufficient discouragement that, in the middle of Greek tragedy, things begin to go badly for the Protagonist – and for the Spectator, who is in tow – and then, just stand by. After a blazing beginning, everything starts to go downhill. Let us call this sudden change of fortune *Peripetaia* – as they say in Brazil, it's always good to name a bull and things become clearer once they're named, more easily understood. So, the tragedy must have two parts: before and after the *Peripetaia*. Before, fun; after, suffering . . . And it must end, for the protagonist, with a corker of a *Catastrophe*, if I may be permitted another technical term, which I will use henceforward.'

'*Castastrophe* for the protagonist, richly deserved, that we understand. And what about the spectators, the audience? What happens to them?' ask the perplexed bystanders.

'They get *catharsis*!' and he gave a shout: 'That's just it: they experience *catharsis*! The spectators have to leave the theatre pu-ri-fied!!!! The tragic flaw – which, if I am permitted, I intend to call *Harmatia* – the flaw is at first stimulated in the audience's emotion, later to be expelled by reason . . .'

'That's all very well, everyone agrees' – said his listeners,

'but . . . at a certain point the audience can unlink itself from the play, when the change of fortunes starts, what Your Honour called *Peripetaia*. They can say – "with me it's going to be different!" Enjoy the fun and go off with the bad example in their memory, the ruinous desire in their heart, without swallowing the moral of the story . . .'

Aristotle, who may have had conservative ideas, but was intelligent to the power of ten, explained his Machiavellian plan:

'Observe carefully: the spectators are *empathically* identified with the *Protagonist*, they think with his head, they feel with his heart. It will suffice if the Protagonist is repentant, if he does a nice big *mea culpa*, and then all will be resolved. This Protagonist's confession I am going to call *Anagnorisis*. You like?'

Everyone liked and, even better, they understood.

'By means of *Empathy* – that precious and indispensable thing, which marries Spectator and Protagonist, and poetically implants in the former the desire of the latter! – the spectators, hearing the confession of the hero, will be making their own confession, promising to themselves never more to err. The errors of the Protagonist will serve to mend the behaviour of the spectator, to un-warp the warped.'

To banish any remaining doubts, he spelt it out:

'Try to follow this carefully: tragedy is the imitation of an action. But to imitate does not mean to *copy*, to *ape* as they say round here: it means to *recreate the principle of created things*. Imitation is a living, dynamic force – not a pale copy. Thus, tragedy goes deep into the spectators' hearts and, through deep emotions, changes their thoughts and those of their behaviours that are unacceptable to society and to those who direct society. Tragedy makes its spectators fit for *social intercourse*. But it is not the spectators who dictate the norms of this social intercourse, it is the prevailing political and economic power through the poetic power of the writer: Solon and the Maecenases.'

So thrilled was Aristotle with his own ratiocination, so convinced, that after this short exchange of ideas he ran home to write a very intelligent book, to which he gave the delightful name of *The Poetics* – a book which I commend to all my readers.[12]

For centuries this text had the status of 'The Official History of Tragedy', a straitjacket on libertarian thespian explosion.

In the cause of truth, I must say two things: first, it is clear that the Greek tragedians didn't all or always obey this *Poetics* – some rebelled. Many died even before the book existed and others took no notice of its precepts. *The Poetics*, however, existed as a model and as an ideal. Second, Aristotle was not given to the sort of rough flippancy I have displayed here; he was a refined person, more given to implication, subtlety and nuance. I, wretch that I am, come from Penha, a working-class suburb in the North of Rio de Janeiro, far from the sophistications of the court. I have to be direct, objective; I can do nothing other than speak the raw naked truth! It is my fate – I am condemned to it.

Centuries later, Brecht, writing on Aristotle, made a suggestion. He began by saying that this history of *Empathy* was good for the dominant classes, who still dominated the ideology of the characters, which ideology, by empathy or osmosis, transferred itself to the audience; but, for the workers, it would not do. It helped to perpetuate exploitation. *Ipso facto*: down with *Empathy* and in its place, take *Verfremdungseffekt*!

What was this, this thing with its exotic name? *Verfremdungseffekt* meant: *seeing from a distance, without involving oneself*. Like a person who observes, thinks and reaches conclusions with his or her own mind. The Actor no longer hides behind the Mask. He goes out and shows himself beside it and contradicts it openly and enters into conflict with the mask. What Thespis did with the Chorus by means of a material object, a mask, Brecht did with the Protagonist by means of *Verfremdungseffekt*.

The duality, which before concretised itself in the contest of Protagonist versus Chorus, now became Actor versus Character. The true *Insubmissive Protagonist* now came to be the *Actor* and the *Poet*, and not the *Character*. The role of *Insubmissive Protagonist* passed from the *Character* back to the *Actor* and the *Poet*.

In the shows of Brecht, however, the intransitive relationship between the stage and the audience still remains. The stage still belongs to the characters and the actors. Even when the Dramatist or the Actor criticise the behaviour of the Character, it is the Dramatist or the Actor carrying out this denunciation, not the audience! By means of songs, commentaries, distance, the Dramatist reveals and is revealed. He exposes his thinking. He does not hide behind the characters and he does not amalgamate himself with them. But . . . the stage continues to be his private property, his space and territory: 'Audience, sit down and just listen to us!'

The immobilised audience member is urged to think of the form of thinking presented as the correct form, the Truth; the person who says this is the Dramatist, who tells us the right way and the Actor who shows it: they state, rather than question. We are far from Socratic *maieutics*, and closer to the Democratic Centralism of certain political parties.

As everyone knows, *all appropriation of speech is an appropriation of power*. Even in Brecht, the dramatist alone appropriates speech, not the citizen. It is true that, at one point, Brecht rehearsed more participative forms of theatre; he pre-cognised the dynamisation of the audience. In some of his poems, he intuited the possible utilisation of the theatre by audience-turned-artists. But, in his great theatre, the wall between stage and audience did not come down.

For my part, I am '*amicus Verfremdungseffekt*', however I think that it is possible to go further – '*Sed magis amicus theatrum oppressi*'.

Not to let oneself to be invaded by the characters is a great advance. So, we should not let ourselves be invaded, that's important. But, is that enough, is that as far as it can go? Must actor and characters continue to dominate the stage, their territory, while I remain immobile in the audience?

I think not. I think that we can travel further along this road: invasion is needful! The spectator must not only liberate his Critical Consciousness, but also his body – invading the stage and transforming the images shown there.

The act of transforming is transformative.

The spectator must *incarnate him- or herself* in the Character, possess it, take its place: not to obey it, but to guide it, to show the path that he or she (the spectator) judges right. All spectators, equally free to experience the liberating seizure of speech, will have the same right, democratically, to expose, by acting (not by talking alone) their own opinions. The spectator must rehearse, in head and heart, strategies and tactics of struggle, forms of liberation.

The *Insubmissive Protagonist* rebelled, separating himself from the Chorus. The mask hid the Actor behind the Character. The realist theatre managed to confound the two, dissolving the actor, who was submitted to the empathic command of the Character. Brecht proposed to separate them anew – Actor and Character – so that the Spectator might be able to contemplate the two at the same time: choose between me and him! But Brecht ended up celebrating the marriage between the Poet (by way of the Actor) and the Spectator, who continued to be lorded over, empathised, as in a marriage in times gone by: the Poet gives the orders, he who holds the truth. The Spectator continued as a bride in the old style.

I, Augusto Boal, want the Spectator to assume her role as Actor and as Artist, to invade the character (and the stage), taking his place and proposing ways and alternatives.

This invasion is a symbolic transgression. It is symbolic of all the transgressions that we have to enact in order to liberate ourselves from our oppressions.

Without transgression (which doesn't necessarily have to be violent!), without transgression of customs, of the oppressive situation, of the limits imposed, or the very law that must be transformed – without transgression there is no liberation. To liberate oneself is to transgress, to transform. It is to create the new, that which did not exist and which comes to exist.

To liberate oneself is to transgress. To transgress is to be. To liberate oneself is to be.

By invading the stage, the spectator consciously practises a responsible act: the stage is a representation of the real, a fiction; she, however, the spectator, is not fictitious; she exists on stage and beyond the stage – *metaxis* – the spectator is a dual reality. Invading the stage, in the fiction of the theatre, she practises and acts; not only in the fiction, but also in the social reality he belongs, simultaneously, to the two worlds, that of reality and that of the representation of this reality which is hers. Transforming the fiction, she transforms herself into herself.[13]

To liberate oneself is to be.

THE SKINNY APES AND PRIMITIVE DEMOCRACY

It will never be known for certain when the first creature, male or female, that we could call a Human Being was born. Was it 100,000 years ago, the era of *Homo Sapiens Sapiens*, or only 30,000 years back, in the Upper Palaeolithic period, when works of art, cave paintings and sculptures, first appear?

In the face of this uncertainty regarding our origins and in the absence of scientific proof, a space is created for poetry, fables and fairy tales.

I have heard hundreds of legends about our first palaeo-grandpa. The one which most enchanted me was from the African nation of Ôbhwa-Ôbhwa, which was told to me personally, by one of its most eminent leaders in return for his own anonymity. So, faithful both as reporter and friend, I keep his name clasped to my heart, locked therein with all keys necessary.

We were seated atop the stump of an illegally felled tree, in a devastated African region to which I had gone as a journalist, with the intention and mission of denouncing such illegal clearances.

The old sage began a leisurely speech, an ancient custom among the old sages. Every now and then he scratched his backside, I didn't know why, right down low. He did a lot of scratching.

He recounted how, thousands of years ago, Africa was a green continent fragrant with lavender, jasmine and damask. A land blessed by God and by Nature, rich in all kinds of banana, *açaí*,[14], *carambola*[15] and other fruits of the forest, growing wild and free: a land veined with refreshing rivers, an open invitation to bathe without a care; a land lapped by succulent seas, in which swam, swift and smiling, all types of fish known to gastronomy.

There were animals of all species, be-snouted and beaked, from the most subterranean of moles to the highest-flying birds.

In the more robust trees cavorted apes, instigating huge nocturnal tumults. In the highest and most magnificent of the trees, however, the famous Imperial Tree, the apes were well organised and civil. There, order reigned.

The Imperial Tree, magically, gave forth fruits of all kinds, from apples and pears to coconuts and pomegranates. The secret of this botanical anomaly resided in the fact that the potent tree, by means of its immense root system, which stretched across the whole continent and even beyond the sea, sucked up the sap of other trees, near and far. So, it was easy.

As we know, in politics it is impossible to please all the people – it's a law of Nature, a law that sticks. The order imposed on this magnificent tree was the reason for the great social stability which reigned there. But not all the apes were satisfied – especially the skinny ones, who were angry about the manifest social differences which existed: while some anthropoids paraded their plump and pink selves, the majority suffered squalor.

An unjust hierarchy created by the branches (it was the branches' fault!) which raised barriers between brother simians, allowing some to enjoy the high life, at the very top, and the majority to suffer, crestfallen, at the very bottom.

My wise old friend unfolded his history, suffering along with these social injustices, and also from the itch on his back.

There was no record, however, of any indication of social unrest. The odd grumbler was heard in the dead of night, the rest were silent. In distant branches, domestic quarrels occasioned muffled cries – just life going on, nothing serious.

The apes believed this inequality to be the work of Fate, in the face of which nothing could be done, or of a Superior Being, against whom arms were not to be taken up.

The apes, as is their irrepressible habit, cavorted about and executed pirouettes in the leaf-laden fronds. From their perches, the ones at the top commanded the simian herd, creeping below. Though they were all of the same pre-hominid race, those at the top seemed to have arms that were long and strong, and swelling chests laden with luxuriant hairy tresses. Those at the bottom, by contrast, seemed pinch-faced and weaselly.

What was the reason for this unjust simian division? Very simple: the fat ones had discovered the way to the larder at the top of the tree in long-forgotten times, before the trees were covered with so many leaves. The skinny ones, oblivious and non-competitive, had never discovered the way to these branches.

The fat ones rejoiced in their privileges: they ate fruits kissed by the sun. When evening fell they could descry from afar the waters of the rivers where the female apes bathed, naked and seductive. They were the first to spot carnivorous predators visiting with aggressive intentions and, last but not least, having sucked the pulp off their mangos and eaten the flesh of their coconuts, they could chuck the stones and the shells down on to the heads of the skinny apes below, in punishment for any less than respectful look. Or just for the fun of it: throwing coconuts down at the heads of others is a pleasing evening pastime – depending of course on your point of view, thrower or target.

For this reason, we can say with certainty that, amongst these mammals, who looked like us and had some of our defects, there already existed a larva of the class struggle.

The fat rulers stated that only by birth could one reach the top, by inheritance, or by special divine decree which no-one knew for certain how to obtain, but that all were obliged to obey, under pain of coconut to the head.

As we know, things seem to be as they are, though they are never as they seem to be. In tranquillity, those at the top ate their bananas with silken sensuality, while those below got the skins.

The thin ones were myopic – as they did not see anything beyond the branches they had in front of their noses, they stayed almost blind, dependants of those with superior knowledge – like in our own times, the fellow who sees the TV, an inch from his nose, and nothing more.

The bolder among the skinny apes had their doubts as to whether this story was being told right. When the old ones went to sleep, after the ceremony of blessing, they stayed up chattering for hours on end, hanging by their tails in the swaying branches, engaging in metaphysical enquiry and asking themselves why the rays of divine injustice shone as they did. If they were all apes in their simian essence, equal or similar in everything – whether gorilla or chimpanzee, orang-outang or macaque, white cheeked gibbon or golden-lion tamarin (different and yet equal!) why should the rays of wrong-headed destiny shine on some, roosting upon the summit, eating mature fruits roasted by the sun, smearing themselves in the honey of queen bees, eating their way through nests and honeycombs, and defacating on those below without a second thought, whilst they, miserable wretches, ate greenery and got a coconut on the head at the slightest hint of discomfort or rebellion?

It had always been thus and we know that everything that has always been thus tends to seem as if always will it be thus. After their ontological and epistemological tortures, the sceptical friends slept. Their doubt endured and Doubt is the seed of Truth.

Divine Justice came in the form of a devastating ecological tragedy. It ordained a pulverulent drought, in which every grain of dust was at least the size of a rocky stone, and sharp and vicious with it.

In the production of this terrifying drought, the hand of God, omnificent, was helped by cows which, ruminating to distraction, caused chemical reactions in their stomachs which in turn produced dangerous and expansive gases. These gases, once expelled with unexampled thunder, rose swiftly to the skies impelled by their explosion and pierced the ozone layer that protected the animals and plants against the mortiferous rays of the sun, infra and ultra.

The sun, which had no thought for anything else, scorched away! It scorched without conscience, by way of official duty, since that is how the celestial bodies act, with no remorse, however much damage they do, with no pity, however many shooting stars are swallowed up by black holes – all in a day's work, for God and the Celestial Bodies.

The aftermath of the drought did not inspire hope – the climate of the whole world transformed . . . the cows were to blame. The sea turned into a dustbowl, crackling dry, fishless, an arid dead sea of chalk, without so much as a tear to moisten it. The green of Africa turned red, a red mixed with bitumen, the smell of burnt petrol and tyres on fire. Leaves fell, leaving denuded arboreal skeletons, and serving as grazing for the famished ants that roamed aimless and listless: they, who professed no religion, had been punished in the same way and with equal fury as the apes.

In the midst of this immense tragedy a new marvel occurred. The humble skinny apes discovered that the fat ones weren't so tall after all – it was pure optical illusion: it was the branches that were tall, not the apes! They were all the same height. All the apes were more equal than they thought, none more equal than his fellow.

This was an immense discovery for the simian community: any ape, however dim, could be at the top – all you had to do was rise. Obviously the apes at the top knew this; no-one, however tells the truth. That's the big truth; there's a lot of lying that goes on.

The ape community was obliged to come down from the trees to seek food. When all ape-kind had their feet on the ground, the subalterns understood that they had been in the habit of looking right in front of their noses, and, for that reason, were incapable of seeing beyond their palm. Now, as they looked at the ground, they had to raise their heads, and look into the distance and discover the Horizon.

The Horizon has the strange property of being always far off, like the happiness of the poor: the more we advance, the more it flees us.

Raising their heads, they discovered the revolutionary nature of looking up at the Horizon, rather than down at your big toe. Many people give up because the horizon moves away, though we know that the important thing is not to get to it: it is to pursue it! In the act of pursuing the Horizon, our gaze ranges far and wide, and we go along finding fruits on our way. No-one sees the horizon by looking at the ground. Look up, people, look up!

In this way it was discovered that all the apes, the high-and-mighty and the rabble alike, all had a head, a torso and four legs apiece! Or were they arms? When you came down to it, why were four limbs necessary for the same task? Would not two or three suffice?

The skinny apes held their chests high, in their happiness. To the amazement of the anthropoid community, when they swelled their breast, their front legs contracted, and transformed themselves into arms – arms being more polyvalent than legs, which were made for the transport of heavy cargo, the whole body. The back limbs reiterated their vocation and lengthened their feet for greater stability. A miracle!

A fantastic specialisation was created: the feet would be used for walking, the hands for handiwork! And the brain increased in size in direct ratio to the amount of time the apes spent looking at the Horizon, creating space for more complex ideas.

The skinny apes democratised the knowledge, explaining: 'You have to feel respect for your selves, brothers! Breathe deeply and you will see your chests inflate: the oxygen will flood your bodies. See how much lighter we feel!'

One of them concluded with pride: 'In the whole of Creation, we, the apes, are the most superior beings!'

Looking at the Horizon, which fled them, some enraptured humanoids knew Doubt, the mother of Metaphysics, and its cohort of anxieties:

> 'Who are we? Who made us in this flawed fashion? Are we the image and semblance of the Superior Being? Are we superior? Whence have we come and where are we going? Is there life after death? Is there life in other forests? What is life? What is the point of living, beyond enabling us to eat bananas? How is it possible that chemical substances, vulgar deoxyribonucleic acids, could be capable of transforming themselves into life and going off walking in that way, as if it was nothing out of the ordinary?'

There was also a practical question to resolve: the drought had been sent by someone. Who was this Hidden Someone who wanted no converse with apes?

'How did we sin?' they asked themselves, aghast. They would have to meet the Hidden One, whoever he was, and ask pardon for any inadvertent sin. Knowing only that the wind moves the leaves – a small stock of knowledge – they needed to understand who moved the world.

This exchange of ideas, chaotic as it was, still stimulated the thinkers. There was only one certainty: a greater Someone existed. In this idea, they placed their faith! How could they meet him? The apes started behaving in an irreprehensible manner, with unimpeachable ethics, incapable even of harming a fly.

Making the most of the ideological confusion, the fat ones who had lost power, sought to regain it. In defence of their prior acquired privileges, they made a proposal:

> 'We need order in this clamour. We should not seek the Hidden One at all times, but sure, we do need to construct a place, a Temple, where every morning we may go to meditate and pledge our goodness, our piety . . . In the temple and there alone. Some of us will be the guardians of this place of Faith and all the others can work during the day, looking for food in the banks of paths or in buried roots, planting okra . . . practical things.'

These words provoked disagreements. Some argued that the recent ecological tragedy had brought forth beneficial consequences: now everyone was working in search of food.

The construction of a Temple dedicated to meditation would bring back the divisions of the past, created by the separatist branch structure – that was the danger. Against the old idea of 'Each ape on his branch!' the revolutionary apes countered with 'All apes on all branches'. Viva the new utopia!

In spite of the overwhelming logic of this proposal, in the hurly-burly of the free-for-all, the fat ones won, because not all the skinny ones had taken up their new freedoms and some were afraid of the fat ones' ugly glares!

The fat ones constructed a Cave with a large auditorium where the common herd would stand, praying. For themselves, they made a long table from behind which they directed acts of worship, atop a platform which raised them high up, as in former times the branches had done. From there, they harangued the masses who came to exercise their Faith in the Horizon, now at designated hours – the rest of the time was for work.

What had been conceived as the Temple turned into the Cemetery of the Faith.

The skinny ones continued to work, but were no longer able to leave the Cemetery-Temple. Out of the corner of their eye, they continued their secret watch on the Horizon. Gradually they went back to the exchange of ideas, not always in a civilised manner, till the fat ones imposed order:

> 'Enough of this excess democracy; all speak and none is heard. We are going to erect a Second Cavern, and vote in some of us so that, inside this Civic Cavern, they can discuss things to their hearts' content, in the name of all, and take appropriate decisions. This is what is called Representative Democracy!'

He or she who stays silent consents. Seduced by the universal right to vote, they voted in the people who shouted loudest, and banged hardest on the table, and cast most promises to the four winds.

This Cavern, destined to be the Temple of Laws, became the Cemetery of Democracy.

The apes who remained outside it had to keep their mouths shut. Of course, they could vote: but what a strange power the vote is – as soon as the electors votes, their power is lost.

The fact of having seen the Horizon from afar, meant that some had developed their cerebral cortex, home of the arts and the sciences, of emotions and thoughts. Now that they were only able to vote in others to vote in their place – they began doing arts.

They painted bison and mammoths on the walls of the caves where they dwelt – and so studied the best way of fighting them; hearing sounds, they began to dance, and to translate what they were listening to into movement.

Till one day, in order to understand life, they began making theatre. Oh no, anything but that – theatre was going too far! The fat apes demanded:

> 'It is impossible to sleep any more with this infernal racket. We are going to construct a Third Cave, an artistic cave: whenever you want to play childish games, go and play in the Third Cave!'

So, what should have been the Temple of the Arts transformed itself into the Cemetery of the Theatre.

Some thin apes, robbed of their faith, robbed of democratic debate and robbed of the fine things in life, became more ape-ish than ever, preoccupied only with eating bananas and making mischief. Happily, others began to believe that the Horizon always has surprises in store for us – not for when we reach it, since we never reach it – but for when we are travelling in its direction: its surprises arise by the way, on the quest for it.

The Horizon cannot be grabbed by the scruff of the neck. Like the dream and like Utopia, it does not exist for us to reach, but as inspiration, for us to pursue.

When they understood this singular truth, so African in its nature, the apes began again to meditate on Faith and on Metaphysics, to promote free and open debate, and to do Theatre and all the Arts, at all times and on any pretext, the better to understand the world.

They did not destroy any of the Temples, but they understood that Faith, Democracy and all the Arts were within them, themselves; within the Apes, and not within the four walls of the three Caves.

I sat stunned by this story – till I was shaken out of my wonder by the Old Sage's challenge to me:

'Why don't you follow the apes' example?' he asked, as he parted from me and went to hang from a tree . . . and only then did I notice that my friend had a tail which he scratched.

ART IN POLITICS AND THE POLITICS OF ART

All human societies present themselves in a *more or less* organised form. In all, we can distinguish certain tiers, each having certain functions, which are *more or less* fixed. Each tier, each sector, each social group, has its own limits and its own goals, which are *more or less* clear.

All social categories are always defined as being '*more or less*' because they relate to real, living, human beings, rather than chemical elements, like oxygen or plutonium, which can be purified in the laboratory.

We run no risk of being pure – however well intentioned our hearts and our vows. Human beings are, by their nature, impure. In this at least, I am a classic Freudian: we are all gregarious porcupines – we feel the imperative necessity of embracing one another, with the inevitable fate of being impaled on one another's spines.

In our societies, we *almost always* find a government of one form or another. *Almost always* we encounter the figure of a leader. *Almost always* we find political parties, or, in their place, an organisation like the *Mafia*, the *Cosa Nostra*: a family linked by blood, arms or dollars.

Human societies are always '*almost always*' and always '*more or less*' and we are creatures of the *herd*, with all the good and all the bad that that implies.

Apart from the leader and the parties, there are other social organisations: unions, churches, neighbourhood groups, professional associations, etc.

The leader is not always of the same type, a single brand. We could however say that, in general, leaders tend to be of an ideological, pathological or zoological nature!

The leader is, by definition, someone possessed of charisma, that much is obvious! All leaders have to have charisma – this is indispensable.

Charisma is a Latin word which means 'gift' and can be of divine or diabolical nature, or can even be only a conjunction of qualities which though exceptional are utterly earthbound. Or, which is worse, charisma can also be related to a serious illness. The dictionary says that, in the Middle Ages, when a person condemned to death suffered an epileptic fit, he was immediately pardoned, because it was supposed that he had received a delayed visitation of Divine Grace, *in quasi extremis*. It is a well known fact that Grace has the power to shake us. Blessed sickness!

Having established this preliminary systematisation of leaders, we can say that an ideological leader is a person who incorporates, symbolises and defends clear, well-defined ideas – and, for that reason, we follow him! He is a person who holds firm positions and never betrays them; a person in whom we can confide, or a person that we can reject and distance ourselves from: but we know who we are dealing with, and how he deals with us.

The ideologically consistent leader is the one who, when asked about the economy, for instance, answers that our first economic duty is to appease the hunger of fifty million people. And, when he makes such an assertion, he is not getting off the subject: he is talking about economics! That's what economics is, for him: rice and beans on the table, with green cabbage, a bit of crackling, and maybe even an egg! That is the economy.

The pathological leader, by contrast, is the chameleon, multicoloured: he is the person who daubs himself with all the colours of all the desires of all the people, and never shows the colour of his own skin. He is the person who threatens to punish thieves, whilst himself stealing to his heart's content! For the right, he snipes at the left; for the left he snipes at the right.

This type of leader does have a coherent language, but it is coherent with all the incoherent segments of society. It is coherent with incoherence! It appears as if this person is always on our side, even knowing that we live in a polygonal society – we have angles in excess. In reality, this leader places himself right in the centre of a circle in which all points are equidistant from him.

The zoological leader, in his turn, is an extreme variant of this fauna. In the centre of Africa, there was a zoological leader who crowned himself Emperor, like Napoleon Bonaparte, in the Cathedral of Notre Dame in Paris, and enacted the most wicked concretion of a metaphor. As we know, all pathological leaders want, metaphorically, to devour those they lead. Sure enough, this emperor pulled off the stunt of taking all the generals who were conspiring against him into a cell, right next to the palace kitchens, so that, once they had been well fed and nicely plumped up, he could eat them roasted with chips. This is pure fact. I never lie! It's not in my nature! Generally in my discourse I prefer not to name names, and for this reason I am not revealing who this cannibal emperor was: I say only, that, with such hunger, he must have had an enormous *Bocarra*![16]

This, by fits and starts, is the function of the leader: to lead. No genuine leader, however, governs alone – an improbable, nay impossible task for a single person, whoever they may be, or come to be. This is where the Party comes in. Some parties, betraying their mission, renounce their function of crucible, of centre of debates and confluences, to become merely a messenger transmitting 'their master's voice', obeying his orders: this is no party; this is the SS.

The true party must always be in a state of healthy ebullition: within it, we must stick to our ideas, which can, to an extent, be conflicting. But, if we are in this party, or in fellow parties, it is because we have desires in common, which outweigh our differences. Some want things to move faster, others don't – but all want to arrive at or close to the same place.

We have desires in common, yes, but how to attain them? Which is the best way, what road should we take? Antonio Machado, the Spanish poet, said:[17] 'Wayfarer, there is no way; the way is made by walking.' Let us walk!

We know what we want, but we don't know how to get it; this is why parties exist, so that ideas may be debated, examined and discussed, and so we arrive at concrete propositions and actions – that's politics, and that's the party. Its function is not to tread narrow, known tracks, following tapering paths over rickety bridges; its purpose is to open up broad avenues along which all can pass! You are right, Antonio Machado, poet! Let's go and penetrate deep into the wood!

The government of a country, however, is not only its leader, nor only his party: the government must include segments of society which place themselves outside it. Government must take these people into account, if it is truly a democracy. Taking them into account does not mean satisfying all their desires – impossible! But we must not transform oppressors into oppressed, and oppressed into oppressors, retaining the oppression with the roles simply swapped. Harmony, up to a point and within certain limits is *more or less* and *almost always*, possible – *almost always, more or less*. Case by case.

Civil society, however, cannot be reduced to leader, party and government – civil society is inscribed in the day-to-day grind of real life, in the beating heart of the people!

The *Porto Alegre World Social Forum*, like other less global forums, is a meeting of citizens and citizens' organisations, which are the soul of society. It is not a meeting of leaders, parties or governments. The Forum has no commitment to govern, but it does have a commitment to make propositions and, when necessary, demands. And where does Art come in, in any Forum?

First, we have to define what Art this will be, because, in Art, as in Politics, there are also leaders, styles, groups and individuals. We, who are of the Theatre of the Oppressed, are a tendency within an Art greater than ourselves, which of course contains infinite contradictory tendencies.

We are those who believe that every human being is an artist; that every human being is capable of doing everything that any one human being can do. Perhaps we may not all do it as well as each other, but we are capable of doing it – not better than others, but each better than ourselves. And every time we do it, we are more capable, and better. I am better than myself, I am better than I think, and I can become better than I have been.

This is what Art is for: we believe that the act of transforming is transformatory. Allow me to justify this.

Sounds are everywhere, whirling around in space, totally random, and all sounds can be remembered, created and recreated in our memory and our imagination: they are real and imagined – imagination being another form of reality. If we organise sounds in time, we are inventing Music, since Music is the organisation of sound and silence, in time. And what are the Visual Arts, if not the organisation of colours, lines and volumes, in space? And what is Theatre, if not the organisation of human actions in time and space? The artist organises the world according to his or her subjective perception – this is our language. The deeper I penetrate within myself, the closer I will be to the Other.

We may now see the meaning of the phrase 'the act of transforming is transformatory'. If I transform clay, potter's earth, grains of sand, and I make a statue with it, I am creating a work of art, transforming reality. And the fact of transforming the sand into sculpture, transforms me into a sculptor. Now I am an artist. If I organise sounds that I hear around me, or listen to in my soul and if I order these in time, I am writing a score; I transform disordered sounds into Song, and the act of transforming the nature of the sounds transforms me into a composer.

If I lay a firm grasp on words that are in the dictionary or run from mouth to mouth, and I order them, as only I know how – I manipulate them, lengthen them, shorten them, change their meaning – if I transform words and meaning and write a poem using them, I am transforming the reality of these words. I am creating poetry and the act of transforming them, transforms me into a poet – one who transforms words.

The same thing happens with the theatre, at least with Forum Theatre, the Theatre of the Oppressed, when the spectator transforms herself into spect-actor, when she invades the stage and creates ideal images of what she wants to come to be reality – her reality. The spectator comes on stage and transforms the images that she sees and does not like – she transforms them into images she likes and desires, images of a just, convivial society.

And the act of transforming reality, even in image, is a transformatory act, since *the image of the real is real at the same time as it is an image*! The spectator, invading the stage, transforms himself into sculptor, musician, poet – in sum, entering on stage and showing his will in action, being the actor, being the protagonist, the spectator transforms himself into a citizen!

From the moment we are conceived, we human beings need to expand ourselves: within and without. Without, by seeking a territory which may be larger than the volume of our body – the house, the garden. Within, poetry. All the poetries. Without, terra firma; within, knowledge and the quest for it.

In Porto Alegre, in January 2003, we are going to discuss the ALCA[18] and its snares, the interest on the External Debt, the urgency of Agrarian Reform, and the monopoly of economic and military power by a single country, which leads us dangerously back towards the 1930s, a decade of unfortunate memories with holocaustic consequences.

However, since we are artists (and, some of us, romantics!) let us use elements of our art, placed at the disposal of all. We will be there, working with the peasants of the MST,[19] with the inhabitants of the poor outskirts of the satellite towns, with members of excluded communities or victims of prejudice, with oppressed of all categories, kinds and natures.

As we are artists, as we are romantics, we believe in that most beautiful phrase of the Cuban poet, José Marti: 'The best way of saying, is to do!' And more: *to be is to do and to do is to be.*

We will never be anything that we will not do: I am a baker because I make bread; I am not an astronaut because I have never been rocket-launched from *terra firma*.

We want to conquer our identity and our citizenship; however, we will only be full citizens if we are capable of intervening in our society – in whatever aspect that does not please us – and transforming it.

Doing art means expanding oneself. Human beings are creators, and each time that they create something, other creations become necessary. Each discovery creates the necessity for other discoveries; each invention begs more inventions.

In the Forum of Porto Alegre, doing art, we will be saying what we think, inventing the society we want, being what we want to be – ourselves.

A LADY IN NEW YORK

When dialogue is initiated, we should never be surprised by surprises. Without surprise, there is no dialogue. 'I think this – Me too!' – is not dialogue, it is monologue *à deux*, chorus, a single voice would suffice.

Forum Theatre is dialogue *par excellence*. We present a scene or a play, in which there is a problem, but not its solution. Then the same show is repeated till a member of the audience interrupts the action and takes the place of the character who does not know how to resolve his or her predicament, improvising alternatives that the *spect-actor* will have imagined. The other actors on the stage or in the performance arena have to improvise their responses, in words and actions.

The whole audience can do the same – so it is only natural that this collective creativity should surprise us every time. Even if the Forum play is repeated a thousand times, even then, every time, someone will say something unexpected, do the unimagined. When the forum begins, prepare to be astonished.

From 1990 or earlier, every year I have gone to New York to do Theatre of the Oppressed workshops at *Brecht's Forum*, at 451 West Street (for anyone who wants to go and visit).

Some time back, I was starting a new workshop there, when, on the first day, I became aware of the presence of a white-haired woman; she was seventy or seventy-five years old, very dignified, haughty even, but she behaved in a strange manner, mostly staring at the walls of the room rather than at me – I swear these walls were not more interesting than my words, or my face for that matter. Her mouth hung slightly open, as if she were smoking a non-existent cigarette in the corner of her mouth, like a cowboy in an old Western.

She did not participate in the games or the exercises. I explained that no-one was obliged to do anything I proposed (that would be oppression!) but that the existence of non-participants in the midst of the group sometimes became uncomfortable, both for the non-participants and for the others, who would feel themselves observed. Unperturbed, the Lady looked at the walls and, to break the monotony of colour, out through the windows at the road and the falling rain.

I imagined that she was paralysed by fear of the work – though without reason: our workshops are gentle and never coercive. In the break, I tried to win her confidence, and I asked her name.

'I call myself Lady!'

I was expecting Mary or Laura, Winnie or Deborah, Sarah, Connie or Michelle, but fair enough: Lady – why not? I asked where she lived. Boston. Was she enjoying the workshop? Yes! Was she tired? No! Did she do theatre? No. There was water, in the corridor, in a big dispenser: Was she thirsty? No. Everything alright? Yes.

I was collecting monosyllables.

When the first day was over, I sought out the director of *Brecht's Forum*, to find out about the strange workshop participant. She said that Lady had told her she had read all my books and was very interested in the introspective techniques of the Rainbow of Desire, the therapeutic techniques, and that her enthusiasm was being roused.

On the second day, I chose some more gentle exercises, always keeping an eye on the enigmatic *dona* Lady. Perhaps only one of these exercises was a little more energetic, when the participants, in pairs, had to push hard against each other, all the while obeying the prohibition against winning: thus, pusher and pushed force each other to use the maximum strength . . . of the weaker of the pair. The result is always a draw, even between unevenly matched players.

I looked for the Lady in the break, to continue my project of aesthetic seduction, but I failed to find her in the corridor, or the other rooms, or by the lift, or in the unheated hallway, where the smokers were allowed to fill their lungs with nicotine.

Where could she have gone? What has become of Lady? She was here. Has anyone seen her? She went that way. She's vanished!

That evening, we telephoned her sister's house, at the New York address she had given us: they answered that she had slightly injured her foot, and was resting and could not come to the phone – this was in the days before the wireless phone or the mobile, as yet undreamt of.

The following day, she didn't appear. We phoned: she was not there. She had gone out and no-one knew what time she was coming back, or even if she had gone back to Boston – who knows, she might have gone to the cinema. We were insistent, and someone promised to pass on the message.

On the third day, the same telephone calls, the same absence, the same 'we don't know what time she's coming back, she went out, without saying where'. We are nobody's nanny but we had this irresistible vocation. In the days that followed, we did not stop phoning, worrying, casting perplexed glances at one other. But in the end, we had done what we could and she had family; she was not alone.

The last day, a cold white Sunday – that treacherous New York cold, when the blue sky makes you think of the beach, and the sharp wind goes right through your clothes and chills the heart – was the day of the Forum demonstration.

I explained the rules of the game. One by one, the various scenes were presented and debated. First, the *model*: a scene which showed a young black woman who was going for a swim with her two younger children, at the local municipal baths. As a resident of the area, she had an absolute, unquestionable right to do so.

But – dressed, as she was, in her swimming trunks – how was she to produce documentary evidence proving her residence? No-one goes to the swimming pool with their rental agreement in hand or bag, nor had she. The white women had no problems; they were asked no questions, but the black woman had to prove her residence. Were the children even hers? If they were, she had to prove it with their birth certificates. Did they have a father? Where did he work? Was she married? Who to? 'Prove it – not because there is any prejudice in this city, that's not how it is here, no way. We are not racists, we are all very liberal – but you do need papers!'

The young woman ended up getting her un-swum children dressed again, and going back home dry. She was seething with anger, but, even so, she had accepted the oppression.

After the *model* there would usually come the Forum, the debate, the theatrical dialogue between the characters remaining on stage and the audience, which would substitute itself for the protagonist, trying all the possible alternatives.

After the scene had been shown, I asked the audience, 'Is this real? Here in New York, even today, at the end of the twentieth century, this type of prejudice still happens?'

Yes, it could happen, and what's more it did happen, and not just once in a while – almost always. I asked:

'Is this a case of inevitable fate, or are there alternatives?'

Sure, there were many alternatives. The audience was wound up, excited. I informed them:

'We are going to start the play again in the same way, with the same actions and the same dialogue: the black woman is going to come on stage with her children and their rubber rings, preparing for their dip. When any one of you has an idea of what she could have done, what she should have done, to break the oppression – since all local residents have the right to swim till they drop! – all you have to do is say – "Stop!" The actors will freeze and the *spect-actor* – because in our audience we don't have spectators, we have citizens, ready to act in defence of their rights' (said I, without excessive demagogy!) – 'the *spect-actor* comes on stage, takes the place of the woman, and improvises the first solution. And everyone else is welcome to follow on after, one at a time, to show, in action, all their thoughts. Is that clear?'

It couldn't be clearer. We went back to the start. When we got to the scene in which the municipal guard asked for the black woman's papers, we heard the door opening with the annoying creak it had, and an aged voice, croaky but strong, rang out:

'Stop!'

It was *dona* Lady – she had come back in the final minutes of the final day.

It would have been enough to throw anyone – what on earth should one do in such a situation? – and I was no exception. I stood there, feeling a degree of fear, but no guilt. Everyone was equally confused, everyone, except her. I set about re-explaining the rules of the game, but I realised she was not even listening to or looking at me. She went on stage and took the place of the woman, who went to sit on the floor, by the wall.

Silence. I waited. More silence. We listened, agog. The silence thickened. It turned solid. Stony silence.

Well, I was the director, so I behaved like one:

'Action!'

She glared at me, furious, and I defended myself stoutly:

'OK: we are going to see the first alternative. The lady, *dona* Lady, can now begin to show what she would do if she was in the place of our young mother! Didn't you hear, I said "Action?"'

'I don't want to show an alternative. I came back to demand an explanation. Who was it who assaulted me – who threw me against the wall, right on the second day? Who twisted my ankle?'

We looked at each other in astonishment, waiting for someone to reveal themselves. But no-one owned up.

'Who was my aggressor?' Her voice was the voice of someone who has just woken up after an overlong sleep.

As no-one was saying anything, I asked her to point out the author of the aggression herself, since I was sure that no-one would have had the nerve to do something like that on purpose, and so whoever had done it, inadvertently, would clearly be ready to ask forgiveness, guiltless though they were. I wanted to promote reconciliation, universal peace.

'Point out the author of this involuntary aggression!'

'I know very well who it was, but I want that person to own up of their own accord. Now!'

Her speech came in shouts, in a voice of powerful intensity, despite her physical fragility.

I did not know what to do. Even on the first day, I was worried that the Lady was a little mad, and now this worry was turning into a palpable certainty. Neither I, nor anyone else in that room, could believe that there was a person present capable of assaulting this fragile, old – I would almost have said, ancient – lady.

I asked if anyone had witnessed the involuntary event. No-one. I asked what sort of assault it had been:

'I was thrown against the wall and I almost broke a rib!'

An inconsistency here: before it was her foot, now it was her rib. I feared that, before long, it would be her knee, head, liver – maybe someone might have gouged her eyes out. I was afraid. I suggested we get back to the task in hand and talk about the accident after the session.

'I want to do it now: whoever assaulted me has to explain why they assaulted me! Why me, why me? And they are going to have to ask my forgiveness, publicly! I am going to pardon them, but I want them to beg for my pardon!'

I had a flash of insight, and I realised that an extraordinary thing was happening there, at that very moment, in front of our eyes: there I was, explaining the workings of Forum Theatre, using an event that had happened in the past to do so, while there and then, in the present, in front of our eyes, a Forum situation was being set up: I was in the middle of a crisis and I didn't know what to do.

I explained this feeling of mine to the group, and asked, nay implored, someone, anyone, to take my place and show me what I should do to resolve the impasse. I waited for someone to come along to save me from this affliction.

The first intervention was by a good-natured Californian woman. She explained to Lady that the accident had happened so involuntarily that even the very causer of the near-broken ankle no longer remembered it having happened. Lady vociferated:

'He is here in this room, he is looking at me now, and he knows very well what he has done, he remembers it just fine, because it was no accident, it was done on purpose!'

The women in the group breathed a collective sigh of relief: it was a 'he', a man, the causer of the tragedy was male. They were safe.

A young man took my place and suggested, as a second alternative, that everyone close their eyes and Lady be given the right to deliver a punch to the aggressor. Even though the person so designated might cry out and we might recognise his voice, both crime and punishment would remain secret. Was this not what the aggressor wanted, secrecy? And would this not offer what Lady wanted, i.e. vengeance?

The noble lady's response was a furious glare. It all had to be done openly, in the light of that overcast day. The public confession was what would constitute the punishment.

The third intervention was along the lines of us ignoring Lady and carrying on with our work without taking any notice of her. Lady glared at us:

'Don't you dare! I'll take on the lot of you!'– she bellowed, imperious at centre-stage.

Somewhat intimidated, we wondered how she would carry through her threat, delivered in such a thunderous tone. But we did not want to put her to the test. At the back of the room, we began to hear weeping from two sensitive and shocked young women, who were even more intimidated than I was. What was to be done? Lady went on, irreducible, demanding vengeance, which would be the mere act of asking her forgiveness.

This was when Ronald stood up, an educated, studious, likeable young man, who had attracted my attention because he never stopped asking questions and wanted to understand everything – he wrote down every word I said and every thought he himself had, filling a notebook a day.

Ronald came forward and I was already preparing to give way – once again, a fourth time – to another spect-actor, when Ronald went right past me, asked me to stay where I was, went down on his knees in front of Lady, and in a very tender voice said:

> 'Forgive me. I thought that neither you nor anyone else had seen me do it. I beg your pardon. It was I who pushed you against the wall with all my strength. I am the culprit.'

So it was true. We were stunned and furious with Ronald – even angrier with him than he deserved, because of all his false charm. And there was I thinking that Lady was mad. Perhaps she was but, in this instance, she was reasonable, sober, positively meek.

> 'Why did you do it, my child? Why? I didn't deserve that. I could be your mother . . .'

> 'I don't know why I did it. I felt a sudden anger. Perhaps because you were not doing the exercises, like everyone else. I don't know why. It was an irrational thing. Suddenly, I was possessed with a desire to kill you. Have no fear, I am no assassin. I knew I wouldn't do it, I could never murder anyone – but I could hurt you, and I did. Sorry!'

'What is your name?'

'Ronald.'

'I forgive you, Ronald, my child. Let's go and sit over there, come, sit next to me.'

They went and sat against the wall, and we were left glued to the spot, petrified, immovable, looking without seeing, listening without hearing, hoping against hope that the nightmare would lift, like clouds clearing. Lady stroked Ronald's hair, he did not know her before the workshops but she behaved now as if he was her youngest child.

'Let's go on' – Lady authorised us, with a soft voice, gently caressing like her fingers running through Ronald's hair.

It was not easy to get going again, but soon we were wrapped up in the search for solutions so that the black mother could go for her swim, and there were discoveries, some more energetic than others, but plenty there were. Passive resistance was suggested when the police came along; going to the swimming pool accompanied by many black friends; seeking solidarity from the white bathers present; taking out legal proceedings against the municipality. In the end, the creativity of the group was inexhaustible.

We were having coffee in the break, when I went up to Ronald, now no longer at Lady's side, and I praised his public confession, at the same time as censuring him for the near criminal act:

'Why did you do that to poor Lady? She is such a fragile woman, such a harmless person . . .'

'Augusto, I didn't do a thing to her!'

'So was that all lies? Were you lying?'

'You didn't know what to do with this woman in the middle of the stage. You asked us to take your place, didn't you? So I listened to your request, and we did a real Forum. I could see that she was not quite right in the head, that she was a little unbalanced and on edge – but it seemed like she needed someone to take the blame somehow for pushing her – which I am sure did not happen by the way, because I was watching her from day one, she fascinated me, and I saw nothing. I killed two birds with one stone: I attended to the director's request; and I attended to her request – and she really wanted to find a culprit. All she wanted was to forgive someone. It was such a small thing . . . A sorry never does any harm . . .'

'Thanks a lot, Ronald: on my own behalf and on hers . . .'

This was the most instantaneous Forum of my life!

Notes

1 Globalisation depersonalises the country, substitutes language, introduces its symbols (Coca-Cola and cocaine, Macdonalds and the Statue of Liberty, all mixed together!) and turns Barra da Tijuca into a sad caricature of Miami Beach. It is easier for them to oppress us if we have their face – a mask or a photocopy (sorry, I meant to say a Xerox) – rather than our own original face, whatever it looked like. If we speak their language and not our own, we cease to be people in our own right.

2 In Brazil, the theatre is transforming itself into television, while television turns into Hollywood and Hollywood into Wall Street! Most audiences go to the theatre to see their favourite TV artists, live TV.

3 So we are told . . . I never actually saw him drinking, I am no eye-witness, I have only read the stories.

4 The finishing point of the parade in Rio de Janeiro's Carnival, and the venue for major concerts in the city. AJ

5 The Eleusinian Mysteries were annual initiation ceremonies based at Eleusis in ancient Greece, for the cult of Demeter and Persephone. AJ

6 Let this statement be clear: this Other that Thespis assumed was not Thespis, but the Desire of Thespis. In this is contained the partition of the I – the I, actor, and the I, character. Both were Thespis! Like today and always: the actor is 100 per cent himself and 100 per cent his character.

7 Literally 'groups of dirty ones', or 'ragamuffin groups', i.e. groups of ordinary participants in Carnival. AJ

8 After Gaius Maecenas, Roman patron of Virgil and Horace, (*b.* 74–64 BC, *d.* 8 BC). AJ

9 The *archon eponymous* was the highest magistrate in Athens, the other two being the *polemarch* and the *basileus*. The Archon of Athens held the post for a year and each year was named after the one elected (e.g. the year 594 BC was named after Solon). Years listed as 'anarchy' meant that there was literally 'no archon'. AJ

10 'O poeta é um fingidor, finge tão completamente, que chega a fingir que é dor, a dor que deveras sente!' From the poem 'Autopsichographia' – 'Self-Psychography'. AJ

11 See *The Legislative Theatre*, where this concept is examined.

12 Apart from the *Poetics* they may also like to read some books of mine, which are also very interesting – the *Theatre of the Oppressed, Games for Actors and Non-actors, The Rainbow of Desire, The Legislative Theatre*, and, if there is any spare time, *Chronicles of Our America, The Suicide who Feared Death, Jane Spitfire*, and, principally, the book in your hands now, reading right to the end! And, most importantly, *The Images of a Popular Theatre*, by Julián Boal.

13 Liberating oneself, paradoxically, the spectator liberates us and allows us to exercise, fully, our art. We have the right to speak because we are capable of hearing. AJ

14 Highly nutritious fruit of a type of Brazilian palm. AJ

15 This fruit exists only in Brazil. AJ

16 *Bocarra* means 'big mouth'. AJ

17 'Caminante, no hay camino,/se hace camino al andar.' Antonio Machado, 'Proverbios y cantares', *Campos de Castilla*, 1917.

18 'Área de Livre Comércio das Américas', or Free Trade Area of the Americas, a proposed agreement to eliminate or reduce trade barriers among all nations in the Western Hemisphere except Cuba. AJ

19 'Movimento dos Trabalhadores Rurais Sem Terra' – The Landless Workers Movement, a large political movement in Brazil, engaged in occupying unused land and making it productive, and campaigning for land reform. AJ

GLOBALISATION, CULTURE AND ART

THE SUICIDE OF THE ARTIST

'Thanks to Your Excellency, now we can choose our own artists', said a happy impresario to the Minister of Culture, at a public meeting, back in 1999, expressing his gratitude for the privatisation of culture.

In times gone by, the patronage of the arts fell to the Minister and the Secretaries, almost exclusively. Today, you go from door to door, cap in hand – whether you end up with a bowl of gruel or a horn of plenty depends on your intimacy with the powerful and rich impresarios. For businesses, delighted to be authorised to use tax revenues for the aesthetic publicity of their products, it is a great deal. For artists, it isn't: let me give my own particular testimony on the subject.

In the year 2000, I directed a fairly large-scale experiment, *SambÓpera Carmen*: Bizet's melodies married to our Brazilian rhythms.

A huge hit. *The New York Times* published a gushing notice, plastered with photos of the show which, according to the paper, was without equivalent in the 150-odd years of the life of this opera – a pleasing exaggeration! The director of the *Festival Paris-Quartier d'Été* came running and invited *Carmen* to be shown in the heart of Paris, at the Palais Royal, in the 1,000-seat summer theatre, flanked by the Louvre and the Comédie Française.

Carmen is the French national opera, *par excellence*: our samba version, in such a prestigious festival, provoked amazement and admiration. Happy, we resolved to start again and we prepared another *SambÓpera*: Verdi's *La Traviata*, in homage to the quatercentenary of the Opera genre, which was born with the famous Peri-Rinuccini *Eurydice* composed to celebrate the French King Henri IV's marriage to Maria de Medici.

A more attractive package, from the publicity point of view, would have been impossible to imagine: we had *samba*, opera, Verdi, Bizet, *The New York Times*, Paris, the Festival. We were sure that the impresarios would be queuing at our door, shouting their offers like traders on the floor of the Hong Kong stock exchange. But that's not how it was.

We went in search of production funds, producing fifty sponsorship packs, stuffed with CDs and musical scores and hopes so strong that they were already certainties. The businesses consulted were ecstatic: 'Boal, you just don't stop, do you – always inventing new things, eh? Amazing! That said . . . sadly the project doesn't really go with our products.'

Businessmen want to sell, what could be more logical. Madness to think that our Violetta, the prostitute heroine who dies of tuberculosis in the fourth act, with her sharps and flats and frequent coughs, could boost the sales of ingredients for *feijoada*. Perhaps we should have gone looking for a manufacturer of penicillin or pneumotorax . . . maybe that was where we went wrong!

Faced with the certainty of further knock-backs, it occurred to me that if businessmen rather than artists are to decide what roads we should go down (whilst also obliging us to sell their merchandise!) then, sooner than we think, our art, which is already tending towards the moribund, will be on the edge of total and definitive decease, ready to be laid in a shallow grave.

How could we speak out against this silent death? Since the fact of leaving artists without support or patronage is tantamount to nothing less than the death of the artist. What use would Picasso have been with no brushes or paints? Or Beethoven and Mozart bereft of piano and harpsichord? Though I do not know how to play any musical instrument, not even the humble *reco reco*,[1] and enjoy no chromatic intimacy with brush or paint, I thought of suicide: *The Suicide of the Artist Without Patronage!*

The Vietnamese example came to me: monks immolated themselves in order to draw the world's attention to the iniquity of the war. Cognizant of the necessities of propaganda, they decided not to die quietly alone in their beds, or drinking hemlock through a straw, like our old friend Socrates. They invented spectacular deaths in public squares, setting fire to their robes in front of TV cameras and photographers' flashes; fifteen minutes of flaming glory!

It seemed to me that *The Suicide of the Artist Without Patronage* would have to follow the same norms in 'lay theatricality' as the acts of those courageous men of God.

In Brazil, however, people go around so weighed down with the task of earning their meagre salaries, running from one job to another, that a man roasting himself in the midday sun would not necessarily attract the interest of the desired audience. So then I started thinking about contracting a small orchestra to draw in people passing close to the suicide: I say 'I' because none of my colleagues, who are usually so steadfast in their solidarity with me – even though they thought the idea was great – none of my colleagues was willing to take on the sacrifice, however much I insisted. They must have had their reasons.

If the music was of too high a quality, perhaps we would have run the opposite risk, i.e. attracting too large an audience. In the event of an excess influx of spectators, it would be necessary to construct a solid platform for the burning person, with banks of fireproofed seating for the avid viewers.

Flames are more attractive and more colourful in the dark of night than in the burning sun. Consequently, our pyrotechnic show would have to be performed after sundown, which would in turn mean we would need to set up twenty to thirty good quality stage lights, at the least.

To run this fine incendiary spectacle, we would need stage hands and electricians, and we would have to contract a good PR agency, to print invitations and a programme explaining the philosophy behind the event – since it had such a philosophy – on good quality glossy paper, etc. And last but not least, we would be short of an excellent producer – which you don't get without money.

We went running back to the *Captadores de Recursos*,[2] a profession invented by the Law of Incentive to Culture: these are specialists charged with making businesses loosen their purse strings, always with an eye to the returns to be had.

To this day, no *Captador* has responded to our request, yet. The marvellous and moving spectacle of *The Suicide of the Artist without Patronage* remains, thus, adjourned *sine die* . . . for lack of patronage. Perhaps it will take place soon after the silent and secret Death of Art and Culture.

Please do not send flowers.

If, however, your desire to support this ultimate funereal homage to our culture in coma should prove irresistible, we suggest the despatch of donations, offers of help, grants, etc. – or simple words of friendship – to any young group of performing artists or painters, asking them to explain why they choose to dedicate their lives to art and culture, instead of more modern activities like the sale of dollars or the Stock Exchange, in this era in which Lucre and the Market God are the most recent incarnations of the golden calf.

THE GLOBALISATION OF THE MUMMIES

As the courses of my life would have it, in the last two months of the last century, I found myself visiting two theatres that I had worked in more than three decades earlier.

In Ouro Preto, in November 2000, a group of students was presenting Greek tragedy. Brave students, unheard-of courage! In 1966, the Arena Theatre of São Paulo had premiered *Tiradentes* there, which I wrote with my brother Gianfrancesco Guarnieri, with music by Caetano Veloso, Gilberto Gil, Theo de Barros and Sidney Miller.

The solicitous caretaker warned me to take care where I trod: I was taking a risk. The floor was in need of repair. The budgets for culture – always the last to be remembered and the first to be discarded – had allowed only the most pressing remedial works to be undertaken.

In December of the same year, I was in the 100-year-old Teatro Juárez, in the historic Mexican city of Guanajuato; in 1969, the Arena sang *Zumbi* there, once again the work of myself and Guarnieri, with music by Edu Lobo. When he finished his account of the glorious revolutionary past of this stage, the erudite guide informed us that he received no wage for his labours: his subsistence was dependent on our good will. There, as here in Brazil, culture exists only thanks to the labours of those who create it. In the metastasis of globalisation, art is not a priority.

Mexico is an intensely religious country, and it is beautiful. Its colonial cities overflow with tourists who, since they cannot buy up the whole country and eat it with chilli and sweet peppers (their innermost desire!) they buy whatever they find for sale, transforming everything into merchandise.

In the eighteenth century Padre Alfato, in a church not far from that theatre, was given to self-flagellation in penance for the sins he might already have committed or might one day commit, so enamoured was he of scourges, especially metal-studded ones. Adjacent to his church he had narrow cells built where sinners could, and still can, follow his example, flagellating themselves, fasting and groaning for eight days on the trot, on payment of a reasonable daily charge which rivalled the rates of a four star hotel.

Stalls sell images of the Virgin and plastic crowns of thorns, which replicate the crown Jesus wore at Calvary, and hurt their wearers in much the same way.

Braided whips were on sale, for the faithful to flagellate themselves with, as Jesus was flagellated by the centurions – this self-service was a sign of modern times. Thus they could pay penance, starting with the exorbitant price of the whips and thorns.

The pretty town of Guanajuato, all the more lovely for its splendid colonial architecture, is known for its mummies. Allow me to explain: by some quirk of geology, the local soil embalms 2 per cent of the cadavers which are buried in it, transforming them into impressive mummies!

Six years after death, according to the law, the coffins are disinterred so that the freshest dead may lie in the same graves, in rotation – the earth and the climate is kind to them in that part of the world! Unless of course the relations can pay a further six years rental – if you have money, everything can be worked out, in that world as in this.

In the face of their chronic economic crisis, many Mexican families, however infinite their love, are not able to afford long rentals, in the long wait for the bones to turn to dust, the fate we are advised and know well awaits them. Enter the gravediggers and they discover that, far from those buried dissolving into the dust of eternity, as they should, many cadavers are conserved in a relatively solid state: fragile Guanajuatian mummies.

What can you do with all these mummies? Burning them would be disrespectful. Throwing them on the rubbish heap, sacrilegious irreverence, for which the perpetrators would pay at the Last Judgement, or even before, if discovered. Turning them over to the families would be the most appalling solution – imagine granny returning to her happy hearth in her new dehydrated form!

God help us! Imagine the children's horror, the neighbours' curiosity, the justified confusion of the police – anything but that!

The respectful Guanajuatians opt for a practical solution, which conforms with religious precepts: beside the cemetery, they have created the *Museum of Mummies, Home to the Cult of Death*, as the poster has it, and there they exhibit the mummies, returned against their will to the society of the living.

I hope sensitive spirits among you will forgive me, but I have to report that among the deceased thus restored to the living world, there is included a foetus taken from a pregnant mummy. I saw its tiny body discreetly laid beside its mother in skin and (mainly) bone.

Thirty years ago, I reverently knelt in the face of death, there exposed in hundreds of exemplars, piled high. In the face of Death, I reverenced life. In that place of prayer at that time, there were no rowdy sensation-seekers – only Mexicans and tourists, awe-struck in front of the mysteries of existence and of finity.

We all know that human bodies are the only matter that has consciousness of itself – prosaically nothing more than that.

I wanted to revisit the same places, in the year 2000. I found kilometre-long queues, winding round many corners. Obediently, I waited: what else could I do? My turn came: I entered. Surprise! Amazement.

I am sure that none of you, gentle readers, will ever have felt fear equal to mine, accompanying children and grandchildren on famous ghost trains, in São Paulo or Florida's Disneyland. I felt fear, terror, panic, shock, horror and shivers down the spine, entering for the second and last time in my life (I swear!) that Train of Death.

Everything in there was reminiscent of a funfair, so packed was it with hot dogs and ice creams and popcorn – there, in that place of worship and respect. Mummies are presented with carved wooden daggers in the breast, in pure horror movie style.

I found myself remembering the old Frankenstein's Monster and Count Dracula films, those mouths dripping with human gore. In that museum, framed as if in the morgue of the Medical Legal Institute, the foetus was still there and just as tiny. It had not grown at all with dead age, but it was now exhibited in a blue-glass coffin – a child! – illuminated with brilliant lights, combined with phantasmagoric music.

The cavernous voices that could be heard through the loud speakers were more ridiculous than the dubbed soundtracks of mystery films on the cable TV channels. I could not bear it. I fled. I left at a run, stumbling over bones, tangling my arms in the plastic spiders' webs on the way.

Once outside, after a few deep breaths, I asked the guide the reason for such a transformation. The man – who even as he spoke to me continued to sell children granadilla sweets in the shape of squalid skulls, and whole skeletons dressed in dark chocolate – explained that for many years the museum was in deficit; the new Management had to make it flourish! The mummies had been transformed into merchandise, like everything in this globalised world of ours.

Once Disneyfied, they were yielding a profit, after six years underground. Death, at last, was being used for something, consumption after consummation.

To ensure that the queues would continue growing and box office takings get fatter, the presentation of the dead has ended up imitating the sensationalist norms of the TV show. Globalisation imposes the same taste on all: we are all equals, the same because we consume the same. We are equal, not as in the proclamations of the UN Declaration of Human Rights or the French Revolution, but because the Laws of the Market say so.

In Guanajuato, homage is transformed into spectacle, and death into a breadwinner.

THE THREE PATHS OF CULTURE

On his election to the Presidency, Lula's first economic projects were to put an end to the starvation of millions of Brazilians, and, in matters of international politics, to extend the hand of friendship to Latin American countries, India, China, Africa; for trade between countries, he suggested barter.

These were very different propositions from those accepted as inevitable in the framework of neo-liberal thought. To be coherent with this new vision of Brazil, Lula's programme for Culture should be equally creative.

It is from our responses to the exigencies of life that culture is born. Culture is the *doing*, the *how it is done*, the *for what* and *for whom* it is done. Beavers always construct the same dams; they are genetically programmed. Sparrows always build the same nest, whilst singing the same song. We human beings have the capacity to invent songs and architecture!

We invent the wheel so we may travel further than our legs can carry us; we invent the bridge, so we may cross the river; we make houses to shelter us, and clothes to protect us from the sun and the cold. Culture is made up of all activities that fulfil needs, even superfluous ones. It is the *way of doing* what is done. *Culture is a vocation of all human beings.* We are all cultural producers, from the stars of our TV to the peasants of Amazonia.

To cover our table we need a tablecloth. Any seamstress can cut out a square of fabric: *hey presto*, we have our tablecloth. A lace-maker from Ceará, however, makes the tablecloth and goes further: the product she makes is art. The lace-maker responds to her own aesthetic needs. Her tablecloth covers the table and pleases the eye. Its value is greater – so great that it may be impossible to use it as a mere cloth to protect the table; this tablecloth itself needs protection.

Art is part of Culture. Culture is the human being. It is that which there is of the human in the being. It is what distinguishes humans from other animals, other beings. Cultural producers, however, do not produce only for themselves. In the act of producing for others, their product becomes a commodity. The artist creates beyond immediate necessity, creating pleasure. And pleasure can become necessary, and it too can become a commodity.

A mortal danger: when artists produce art, they are responding to their own way of feeling, seeing and thinking. When their art is transformed into a commodity, external demand is introduced as a priority. Art, transformed into commodity, faces the challenge of the rigours of competition and the rituals of the auction. The artist is responding no longer to himself, but to the demands of a market led by propaganda. The vocation of culture becomes a profession.

In an Exhibition of Indigenous Art, in São Paulo in 1990, one of the exhibitors confessed: 'In our village we make statuettes without the bright colours we paint them with for the *paulista*[3] market – the buyers prefer the coloured ones.' This First Nation man was an artist, being turned into an artisan, repeating ready-made accepted models. Before, he was making indigenous art; now he had moved on to making art for the white man. The laws of the market are the laws of the merchants, just as the law of the wild is the law of the lion.

Culture is also a Profession. In the globalising process, culture and art come to serve the same purpose as commerce in general, i.e. profit, propaganda and the depersonalisation of the artist. Hollywood devours everything and turns it into homogenous "produce" for the globalized market. We have to protect our own industry of Culture because in some way it shows our own identity.

To fight for our cultural life, we have to study our past, in this fantastic present we are living through, in order to be able to invent our future: which takes us to the third strand of an innovative cultural plan: *Culture as Memory of the Past and Invention of the Future.*

Culture is no luxury: it is me, it is you! It is the man in the street, the people in the square – 'The square that belongs to the people, as the sky belongs to the condor!'[4], the poet Castro Alves wrote!

Notes

1 A musical instrument made of a piece of bamboo with notches cut into it and over which a rod is rubbed to produce a rhythmical sound. AJ

2 Literally, the fund lurers or resource capturers! AJ

3 Relating to São Paulo. AJ

4 'A praça! A praça é do povo, como o céu é do condor'. Castro Alves, 1847–1871, Bahia-born poet, who often compared his poetry with the flight of the condor. AJ

THEATRE IN PRISONS

KING CLAUDIUS'S CROWN: OPPRESSED AND OPPRESSORS

Oppressed and oppressors should not be naively confused with angels and devils. Neither one nor the other exists in a pure state. From the beginning of my work with the Theatre of the Oppressed I have on many occasions been led to work with oppressors in the midst of the oppressed, and also with some of the oppressed who were themselves oppressing others.

In 1977, working with peasants in Sicily, in the South of Italy, we were preparing a play in which the Mayor of the city of Godrano was shown as a great oppressor of the poor. During the Forum Theatre show, the Mayor himself appeared in the square and asked to take the place of, not the oppressed protagonist as is customary, but the character of the Mayor – i.e. himself – the better to justify his actions.

The Mayor knew full well what he was doing; his hostile actions and right-wing arguments, on stage, merely reinforced the peasants' beliefs about him in real life. Since he knew what he was doing and how he was doing it, this oppressor could not be changed, nor could he change himself, into something he neither was nor wanted to be; he was aware both of the wrong he was doing and the benefits he was drawing from it. Working with this man would have been a pointless waste of time, pure foolhardiness. Fighting against him, however, was indeed well worth the trouble, and he was defeated in the next elections.

There is also the oppressor who knows what he is doing but defends himself saying that he has 'no other way out', in spite of not agreeing with what he does, he says he is obliged to do it. An example of this would be the policeman who shattered my knee in a routine torture session, in 1971, and asked my forgiveness every time he turned on the electricity:

> 'I do beg your pardon, I have nothing against you personally, I have the greatest respect for you, a genuine artist – but this is my job, I have a wife and kids, I need the wages, I have to work and . . . you just happened to turn up on my shift . . .'

Nothing can be done with cynical people like this, just as nothing could have been done with those low-ranking police officers in occupied Europe during the Second World War, who rounded up their victims and handed them over to the Gestapo, so that they could be killed in Nazi concentration camps. They too argued that they had families and needed their wages. And, after all, the victims were *only* Jews, communists, gypsies and homosexuals . . . of little importance.

People like these – the ridiculous apes of Pinochet and other bandits – cannot be let off with the argument that they are 'the product of a society', since they were brought up in societies which also produced ethical people. No society mass produces its citizens – we are all responsible for our acts.

A number of times I have heard the shameful argument that even 'Hitler was not born a monster, it was society that turned him into one'. I think, on the contrary, that we cannot pretend not to know that we have free will and that we are responsible for the choices we make, each of us, within a concrete social and political situation – a situation which is powerful and determinative, but not to the exclusion of all choice. The History of peoples and the Biography of individuals is not the work of Fate. We construct our lives, lives which are not written in the lines of our palms, to be read by a gypsy.

We cannot grant forgiveness and offer our amity to a person who has chosen personal profit at the price of the unhappiness of others, and decided to enjoy his or her own life at the cost of other people's deaths. Those who want to forgive everyone, 'to see both sides of the question', or 'to see the question from all sides', those who try to justify the oppressors' rationales for their actions – these are people who want to stop History.

If it were true that everyone has their reasons, and that all these reasons are of equal weight, then it would be better that the world stay as it is. We of the theatre of the oppressed, by contrast, want to transform the world. We want it to change, always in the direction of a society without oppression. That is what we mean by 'humanising Humanity': we want mankind to stop being, as the poet Plautus put it, 'the wolf of man'.

We know that all societies advance by means of conflicting structures: how could we, then, assume a position of virginal *exemption* in the face of conflicts of which, whether we like it or not, we are part: we will always be allies of the oppressed, or accomplices of the oppressors.

Doing Theatre of the Oppressed is already the result of an ethical choice, it already means taking the side of the oppressed. To try to transform it into mere entertainment without consequences, would be to disown it; and to transform it into a weapon of oppression, would be to betray it.

It is true that the Joker in a Forum Theatre session, for instance, must maintain his or her neutrality and try not to impose his or her own ideas, BUT *only after having chosen his or her camp!* The Joker's neutrality is a responsible act and arises after having made a choice, after taking the side of the oppressed; the substance of the Joker is doubt, seed of all certainties; the end is discovery, not abstention.

Let me give two very simple examples, and I am sure that everyone will understand:

1 In a conflict between David and Goliath, neutrality means taking the part of the oppressor, the giant Goliath; if we wanted to take the part of the oppressed David, we would have to help him find stones to throw.
2 For those who are religious, I want to note that not even God, in the Last Judgement, remains neutral; he bases his judgement on a Table of Values.

Following the divine example, even we, mere mortals with our days numbered, even we must have our Table of Ethical Values – we have to be clearly on the side of the oppressed and not on *all* sides, in the theatre as in our life as citizens.

Using as our point of departure the clear taking of a stance in relation to the issue at hand, and only after having taken that stance, we will then be neutral in relation to all the oppressed participating in a TO session: we have a duty to hear everyone and to try to understand the meaning(s) of all their interventions; Then, yes, we can look at each situation from all sides.

To work with the oppressed is a clear philosophical, political and social choice.

This choice can be motivated by an *ideology*, which is one of those umbrella words which can embrace a variety of meanings. It was proposed first by the French philosopher Destutt de Tracy (1754–1836), who attributed the origin of all human ideas to our sensory perceptions of the external world, not necessarily in a conscious manner. According to the dictionaries of today, it can also mean:

1 A set of ideas present in theoretical, cultural and institutional spheres of societies, which is characterised by being ignorant of its origin in the necessities and interests of the economic relations of production and, moreover, ends up benefiting the dominant social classes.
2 A set of ideas and convictions which, consciously, directs the actions of an individual or a social group.
3 A set of norms and objectives predetermined independently of each concrete situation, generally attributed to the dogmas of a political party, sect or religion.

So we can see that the Theatre of the Oppressed has nothing to do with this last definition of the word *ideology*, which is the common usage, since we consciously distance ourselves from all political or religious dogmas. But equally we should never lack the conviction and determination of the second definition, so that we may fight, effectively, against the first.

In the examples cited I have spoken of antagonic oppressors, against which there is nothing to be done, other than fight: both their arsenal and their strength need to be destroyed, in order for the oppressed to liberate themselves. No argument can justify collaboration with enemies such as these.

This is not a topic for theatre: it is a duty of citizenship!

There are some people who, either by culpable naivety or out of cunning opportunism, use some scattered elements of the arsenal of the Theatre of the Oppressed dissociated from its philosophy, and let themselves be contracted by commercial or industrial companies to work with their employees. The grave offence is not in being contracted by a business to do your own work, your own project with the groups of your own choice, but in not recognising that these businesses will never permit on their premises – and still less, with their finance – the freedom of expression that the Theatre of the Oppressed demands and without which it withers. If they pay for theatre work it is because they want to improve the productivity of their employees and staff, or to resolve problems to do with relationships, in order to increase their profits – which is perfectly within their competitive logic. They pay for and buy a service as if it was merchandise – and any theatre practitioner who goes down this road thereby transforms themselves into merchandise.

In order to justify themselves, some affirm that, since the Theatre of the Oppressed was first born and developed in poor and under-industrialised countries in Latin America, an adaptation to 'more sophisticated societies' becomes necessary – an argument which demonstrates either congenital bad faith or voluntary myopia.

All human societies are complex: what can be simple(-minded) is the way people perceive them. Some people are incapable of seeing, feeling and understanding subtleties existing in other cultures – cultures which are not their own – or even in their own culture. And, if they do not see them, they state that they do not exist.

Even when the evidence is staring them in the face, there are those who do not see that the world is being more and more dominated by the Dogmas of the Market Economy – the great God Market takes the place of all other gods! Its hunger is for profit. All over the world, the rich are getting richer and the poor are getting poorer. African countries, decimated by AIDS, are obliged to pay never-ending interest on their debts, even at the cost of greater slaughter. Profit is what matters, dividends: human life is worth nothing, and the dead do not register on the accounts!

In the face of the Market and of Profit which, in the globalised world, take the place of all the values called 'humanist', we have to take a stance, which is philosophical, political and social – action! We cannot float above the World we live in, seeking to understand everyone's reasons cosmically and trying to justify all, both those who exploit and those who are exploited, masters and slaves.

Our taking of a theoretical position and our concrete actions should not arise from the fact that we are artists, but because we are human beings. We may be vets, dentists, masons, philosophers, dancers, teachers, football players, judo fighters – but, whatever our profession, we have the citizen's obligation to place ourselves on the side of the downcast and the injured.

We are *living beings*: we need air, water, and land. The air is polluted by smoke, the water contaminated by industrial waste, and the earth surrounded by barbed wire and walls. And so what are we to do? Are we to say nothing? We are *social beings*: in the world outside, bellicose countries armed to the teeth impose their will on others, they invade, they enslave – the Rationale of the Prince is his Power! Night is falling on the world. So what are we to do? Remain silent?

I have sincere respect for those artists who dedicate their lives exclusively to their art – it is their right or their condition – but I prefer those who dedicate their art to life.

The Theatre of the Oppressed was never an equidistant theatre which refused to take sides – it is the theatre of struggle! It is the theatre OF the oppressed, FOR the oppressed, ABOUT the oppressed and BY the oppressed, whether they be workers, peasants, unemployed people, women, black people, young people, old people, people with mental or physical disabilities – in the end, all those on whom silence is imposed and from whom is taken the right to a full existence.

There are also non-antagonic oppressors, with whom careful dialogue is possible, and also relational transformations.

In Santiago, Chile, in 1974, invited by the French Consulate, I worked with Chilean workers; amongst them, a person who was amongst the most combative in the struggle against the dictatorship, proposed a family scene in which, unconsciously, he showed himself to be a dictator towards his wife and daughters. In politics, he was struggling against the dictatorship, and in his family, he was exercising dictatorial powers.

This worker was unconscious of the oppressions that he was carrying out, since, for him, they were the only way he knew of 'being a good strict father', and a way he accepted. He was confusing the oppressive choices he was making with the *function* of Father. He was as unaware of the meaning of what he was doing as the prison guard who, after a Forum Theatre session on the violent behaviour of prison guards, commented: – 'I did not know I was a torturer: I thought that what I was doing was *educating the prisoners.*'

Both guard and worker learnt something about ethics and, for sure, they changed their behaviour. They were unconscious oppressors and, in part, they stopped being so. It was worthwhile working with these people and could be transformatory.

Someone may find it strange that I condemn the torturers in the beginning of this article and now I say that some of them may be pardoned. But, pay attention – there is a big difference between them, which I illustrate with the scene of King Claudius after he is discovered and denounced as the murderer of his own brother, the old King Hamlet. Praying to God, asking His forgiveness, Claudius himself understands that he cannot be forgiven. Why? He explains:

> 'My fault is past, but, O, what form of prayer
> Can serve my turn? "Forgive me my foul murder"?
> That cannot be, since I am still possessed
> Of those effects for which I did the murder –
> My crown, mine own ambition and my queen.
> May one be pardoned and retain the offence?'

Those who commit crimes cannot pretend to be pardoned at the same time that they keep the profits of their crimes and go on committing them. If we pardon these, we are condoning their crimes and being their allies.

In the Centre of the Theatre of the Oppressed in Rio de Janeiro we have worked with men who beat their wives. The shame that some felt, on seeing themselves on stage, was already the beginning of the path towards possible transformation. Some would say this is a small thing. Yes, tiny, but *the direction of the journey is more important than the size of the steps.*

We have worked with teachers who beat their pupils and fathers who beat their children: the theatricalisation of their oppressions shamed these oppressors and, for many, changed them. The Aesthetic Space is a magnifying mirror which reveals behaviours that are dissimulated, unconscious or hidden.

We must never be afraid or ashamed of working with people who perform functions or jobs which offer the opportunity and the power to oppress – we have to believe in ourselves and in the theatre.

But we must take great care . . . and know how to choose which side to be on.

THE FREEDOM OF PROMETHEUS AND THE SOUND OF SILENCE

I have never done theatre in prisons; except when I myself was imprisoned!

In 1971, for a month, I was in a maximum security cell, separated from the world by two iron doors – a dungeon. At that time, I was very dangerous, I struck fear into the hearts of the constituted authorities.

Behind bars I discovered I was not my own master – I decided nothing, I did not have Free Will, that precious gift distributed so liberally by God in his munificence – whenever he can. In my cell, I was unable to plan the minute, the day or the future. My *tomorrow* would be the same as my *today*, which was no different from how my *yesterday* had been. My body was imprisoned – but not my imagination!

Within the walls of my cell, I regained freedom: a certain freedom. When free in space, we are prisoners of time. Those who are prisoners in space, become free in time.

On the outside, in the repeated grind of daily life, the day-to-day routine did not allow me to see myself – I was in a hurry. In my cell, I was obliged to look at myself and see myself. When I had space, I had no time. Now I had time, and lacked space.

In this diffuse disintegration of time – always *now*, with no *before* or *after* – I thought about myself. For the first time, I heard the sound of silence!

And the silence told me: 'In every moment of our lives, each and every dense, profound moment – when Life and Death meet and look each other in the eye, when they rub against one another and sparks fly – time is, at one and the same time, a single second and an eternity: nimble time, consumed in fleeting thought, and stretching out eternal in lasting emotion. I understood the infinite: it is the meeting of all times within the same space.

In my cell, I sought myself out and I asked: who am I?

For the leaders of the coup, I was an impurity which had to be removed from the social order, so that the world might be purified of my existence and inconvenient presence. For me, my only mistake had been how little I had done: had I dared more, I would have done more.

Even though I was innocent and my jailers guilty, prison suspended me in time and confined me in space.

They could raise mountains around me and bind them to my chest. They could shackle my feet and bind my hands but my thought was free, like that of Prometheus bound.[1]

In the prison cell, my body was imprisoned, but not my memory – and still less my imagination. Walled in, my thought was of alternatives. What lives might I have lived and didn't?

In the Theatre of the Oppressed, the citizen, in the present, thinks about their past and invents their future. The stage of the theatre – like the cell or the prison yard – can be a place of study, of appraisal; and theatre can be the language of this search for the self.

Prison can be a time of reflection, a space of learning, a place of discoveries. In hospital, the sick body is not immobilised, in order that, by itself alone and by miracle, it may heal. The body can be attended to, in both situations: in hospital, by the doctor; in prison, by the educator and the artist. If the former uses medicine, the medicine of the latter can be theatre.

Theatre is *the representation of the real*. This representation of the real – reality, in itself! – is a laboratory for research, experiment, analysis. In these representations of the real, one looks at the circumstances in which the offence or crime was committed. One can analyse the act which caused the punishment and the society in which it was carried out. One can rehearse alternative modes of social relations and re-invent the human being!

The prison cell cannot be *life on hold*. The bear hibernates. When it awakens in spring, it is the same bear that went to sleep in the autumn. The prisoner – supposedly – when he released, after his 'cure', should have been turned into someone else, and should not go on being the same bear that went into prison, after his crime.

But how will it be different if the prisoner-bear has only hibernated? In Brazil, we have the death penalty. The outstanding debts are wiped out, not the whole man, but part of his life: the time of his punishment. A citizen from the age of 18 to 30 is wiped out!

If, beyond the prison walls, there is a social structure – even a sick one, which produces delinquents! – then within those walls there has to be a social organisation, rather than a depository. In prison, one is preparing the return to social life, to society. This return to the world outside needs to be rehearsed inside the walls.

Education – Paulo Freire, present and correct! – is transitive. Learning is an act of life: when anyone discovers anything, they are discovering themselves and discovering the other. The act of learning creates a human being different from who he or she was: a person who knows something he or she did not know before.

Prisoners need to comprehend what they have done and what they have to do, and they need to rehearse ways of living in society.

The medium which can best fulfil this task of teaching by concrete life examples, by acts and actions, is the theatre. And the theatre that can enable the spectator to transform himself into a protagonist is the Theatre of the Oppressed.

ETHICS AND MORALITY

The speech which follows was delivered originally in December 2002, in a presentation of a new program to be implemented by CTO within that part of the judiciary system that deals with young people 'in conflict with the law', as they are officially designated. Representatives of many state and national authorities were present, along with prison staff and other guests. I wanted to be honest about our intentions, encouraging about our projects, and suitably proud of the efficiency of our Method.

I explained that our theatre was not mere pastime, but also that we did not intend to explode the structures of the prisons. Our desire was neither to terrify, nor to tranquillise.

The Jokers of the Centre of the Theatre of the Oppressed – the people who actually made our prison projects happen – were all present: Bárbara Santos, Helen Sarapeck, Claudete Felix, Geo Britto, Olivar Bendelak, Cláudia Simone, Luiz Vaz. It was they, and they alone, who took on the risks of the experiment.

Here is the text of my speech:

Rarely in the history of Humanity has it been so easy to discern the secret intentions behind empty words, as in the ingenuous and menacing transparency of the official discourse of today. Brute force is the only value. The UN is turned into a fine pulpit for ornamental rhetoric. Each nation may do as it pleases, if, of course, they have the requisite quantity of tanks and bombs for the job. Terrorism is fought with state terrorism; religious fanaticism, with fanatical bellicosity.

We have to close our eyes to avoid seeing that the real world is suffering agonies worthy of our childhood nightmares. These days, I am happy when I have a nightmare, as relief from what I see when I am awake. In sleep I pray for nightmares, like grass prays for rain: I need them for my psycholological equilibrium and to cultivate the hope of, one day, awakening.

We need the sense of security lent us by those monstrous dragons that used to hide under our childhood beds and strangle us with their sweet sadism, all the while smiling flames; healthy squint-eyed phantasms hidden in wardrobes, in the attic and the cellar, that suffocated us, sensually; witches, flying on broomsticks, treading on clouds – healthy nightmares! In those days, after a restless sweaty sleep, we awoke.

Today, who will wake us from our daylight nightmares?

El Niño promises typhoons, tornados and storms, if we do not sign up to the Kyoto protocol, which no polluter is doing; the price of oil could fall, but for that to happen Iraq needs to be destroyed – which is the solution proffered by the corporations engaged in the reconstruction of the Babylon of King Hammurabi who, ironically, was the inventor of the Law, almost 4,000 years ago, as well as being king of the country that invented the wheel.

A race that does not love another race, even though they are both the same race; a god who does not love another god, even though both are the same god; a nation that does not love another nation, even though both are the same State – all of these have the right to cut the throats of their fellow men; being strong, they can destroy without compunction – crushing persons or entities that could one day be their fraternal friends.

This is the Morality of the world.

There is no Ethics in the prevailing Morality. Nothing of what is said is true, and the truth is never voiced. A society without Ethics breeds offenders because it itself offends.

In the film *City of God* there is a twelve-year-old-child who knows what he wants: 'I want to rob, kill, and snort coke, because I want to be respected!' Where did he absorb this Code of Ethics whose values are so coherent, so logical, and so monstrous?

When a society disintegrates, the values on which it is founded dissolve and fragment. Its institutions remain, but no longer have the functions that gave them their origin. We make the mistake of using words in their old meanings, when new realities are camouflaged behind them.

Family: the paternal and maternal figures should be continent protectors. In the ranks of the poor, it is common enough for a father – maybe alcoholic or unemployed – to order his son to rob, and then demand his share; or for a stepfather, an uncle or a brother, to rape an adolescent girl in the family. The mother works herself to death, in the home and out at work. Many *families* drive their children from the very home which should be their refuge and the formative nucleus of their character.

Eighty percent of poor children interned in our reformatories have been to *school*, but *school* devoid of its pedagogic function. Teachers receive a salary one tenth of the minimum needed for a life of study and dedication. How can they teach?

With no family support, with no access to education, the street is open and inviting – '*Lady, you got some change for me?*' – '*Get out of here kid, before I call the cops!*' The *Lady* never sees the child: she sees the danger he represents. – '*Lady buy some of my chewing gum!* – '*I won't – your parents are exploiting you.*' – '*Lady, give me your gold watch . . .*' – says the young man pointing a gun. She obeys.

The drug-trafficking business, which is highly organised, creates its own morality, without any goal beyond the immediate action. No meaning transcends its acts: Morality without Ethics, *Mores* without *Ethos*.

The drug-traffickers shelter the young and offer them opportunities in crime: all they have to do is rob, kill, and snort coke – and they will be respected. The traffickers intimidate and organise the community: they are school, religion and family in one, and of course, career – short though it is, usually ending in your twenties.

Here you learn, like at school. There are strict rules, like in the army. The total surrender of body and soul is required, like in the church, and amusements are laid on, like in samba. Drug-trafficking is a game of life and death, like football, and it can allow a rapid rise in life, as elsewhere in the neo-liberal world.

The world of drug-trafficking is attractive – let us be frank. If you respect its laws you are guaranteed your place, your ascent through the echelons of crime. If you do not respect them, even if you are seven years old, you get shot in the foot or a bullet in the neck, just like in that film.

Most of the young men and women participating in our project were part of one or other *Comando*[2] of the narco-trafficking network. Their perceptions of the world and its values were intransitive and unquestionable. They got given peremptory orders and they obeyed. In the reformatory, this vision of the world is confirmed: the youngsters meet the same authoritarianism, drop their heads and take the knocks.[3]

The young people need to help to construct, aesthetically, images of their reality – past and present – and, later, to construct future, ethical worlds, in the subjunctive mood – i.e. *'what if . . .?'*

Young people in a judicial educational establishment cannot just be confined and left to their own devices, under pain of lifelong embalmment.

If the youngsters can see nothing in front of them but a white wall spattered with blood, if no intelligent activity is offered them, they will be condemned to fall into the quicksand of ideas and values incorporated in the drug-trafficking business.

Fractures and ruins

Our society is a vast network of organised crime, which reduces 50 million Brazilians to hunger. This *is* organised crime: people are starved, legally, in a country which is the eighth largest economy in the world.

This should not lead us to despair! It should stimulate us to reconstruct our society and make it Ethical. We have to understand that those youngsters had no other choices, or could not see them. They are victims.

Is this a *fracture* in society? A point at which our social structure is torn or a wound in the healthy body?

A business disrespects its workers' rights: a fracture has occured – TO is done to organise the strike and demand respect. A *latifundiario*[4] expels the peasants from land he has stolen: a fracture! Theatre helps us choose ways of making appropriate responses to these social fractures.

What we are seeing in Brazil is not *fractures* but *ruins*, the *remains* of societies that have been torn apart, where no paradigms exist. *Wrong* does not exist because there is no *right*. The Morality which prevails – *moral*, from the Latin, *mores*, 'customs' – is on a collision course with Ethics – from the Greek, *ethos*, goals, objectives, values to which we aspire! *Mores* is what is; *Ethos* is the tendency to go where one is not yet. *Mores* is past and present; *Ethos*, present and future! Morality refers to that which is commonly accepted; Ethics refers to that which we want to come to be.

In its day slavery was considered Moral, just as the *latifundio* is today; no-one was astonished at the idea of a rich man owning slaves, just as today few people are astonished that 1 per cent of the population should own 50 per cent of our cultivable land, and that the richest 10 per cent should wield 90 per cent of the economic power of the country, and the poorest 90 per cent, only 10 per cent.

In the face of slavery, no-one felt the need to give any explanation: it was simply the prevailing morality of the time, just as poverty and hunger are today in this very rich country, and all around the world. By contrast, the ethical stance foresaw Abolition as we today foretell Agrarian Reform. Those who can see this are ethical beings, rather than merely moral creatures.

The complexity of theatre work in prisons

When we work with social groups whose ethical values we share – MST peasants, Teachers' Unions, poor communities, black people oppressed for being black, and women oppressed for being women – with these groups, we establish a fraternal partnership. Our function is to help them; our politics is to support their politics. We do not question their values because they are our own.

In the adult prisons, or the reformatories for young people, the contrary is the case – we have partners who have committed acts we do not approve of. With these partners, we cannot identify, though we may be able to understand them: we have not committed any crime or offence, but we are capable of working with those who have done so and are now paying the price.[5]

But it is necessary for the prisoners to *rectify their values and their goals* – we do not want to help them to commit the same acts that led to their confinement.[6] *This rectification of ethical values is indispensable.* To our great joy, this has happened on occasions.

To see an act carried out, on stage, is the best way of understanding that act in all its ramifications, the best way of imagining the future and preparing for it.

Our work, however, cannot be successful unless we also achieve real changes in the prisoners' conditions: when a cell intended for twenty prisoners is crammed with more than a hundred, there is no aesthetic that can lessen the effects of this ethical crime.

When we work with prisoners our relationship is bi-polar: us and them. In this *bi-polarity* there arise contradictions between *ethical values* and *moral behaviours*. When we work with educators and prison guards – even if not in the same space, or at the same time – this relationship becomes *triangular*. The contradictions multiply and we have to take into account the four Ethical Codes which get entangled in the complexity of these structures.

First, the Code of the agents[7] of the penal system. We have to see, theatrically, how they comport themselves in the prison, but also how they behave in other relationships in their daily lives. In which aspects of their lives the *guard* function orients and monopolises their actions and thoughts. *Guards*, in prison situations, cannot be limited only to their function – of guard – without being able to question it.

Just as prisons are not human rubbish dumps,[8] so the guards are not doorkeepers of Hell: they have to be educators, teachers, counsellors and friends. That said, the majority of the guards take this job only because there would be no other on offer. Many have a horror of their work and feel like nurses treating lepers, with no gloves to protect them.

However, it is they who have the most intense contact with the prisoners, their necessities and anxieties. We have to help the guards to dignify their profession, since its function is to assist the transition between prison and freedom. *Guards* should have a noble function, like *doctors* and *teachers*.

The revaluation of their profession must be our first priority. If a guard inflicts dehumanising treatment on a prisoner, it is the guard himself that is dehumanised. To do is to be! I am what I do! If I torture, I am a torturer – that is, I become less than a human being.

We have to suggest situations in which the guards find themselves in the condition of *oppressed*. It is essential that they experiment with being on both sides, even if not in the same situation.

Second, the Ethical Code of the convicted criminal, which contains the prisoner's own legitimate desire to be someone – to be respected, like the child in the film said. This code has to be analysed so that the prisoner can understand it through another prism, and place his own values against those of a different Ethics.

The time spent in the prison should be a time of learning, rather than a school of crime. The deprivation of freedom in space should intensify the appreciation of freedom in time.

If the prisoner is not allowed to expand his culture and get to know that of others, this deficiency is equivalent to offering no medicine to a patient in hospital.

How will the convicted criminal be able to separate himself from the stigma of *convict*? How will he avoid his face changing into the mask it has been covered with? Once the sentence is done, the debt paid, the stigma of *convict* should not follow him to the end of his life, like a cattle brand bearing the mark of the owner.

Our work with the prisoner must look forward to his possible life, after prison. We have to use theatre to deal with his present oppressions, in the prison, and to conjecture his future oppressions, in freedom.

Third, the Polymorphous Ethical Code, prevalent in our society, must be critiqued. We have to expose the crimes that this society which doles out the punishment commits itself, with impunity.

When people speak of *social reintegration* we have to be careful to make sure that this is not a matter of putting the ex-prisoner back into the same unhealthy environment where the outrage or crime was committed. Reintegration should be transformatory: changes have to be made *on both sides*. If not, inevitably reintegration will be followed by reoffending.

Fourth, our own Ethical Code leads us to ally ourselves with the oppressed – prisoners,[9] guards, civil servants and families – whose right to dialogue is limited and on whom is imposed a coercive monologue.

We are not judges – but we have our Code. How can we avoid manipulating our partners with it, imposing our vision on them?

Some prisoners can persevere in the same options that brought them to prison: we have a duty to reject subject matters and processes which might feed this tendency. Not in an authoritarian way, but by maieutically asking questions about possible alternatives.

This confrontation of Ethical Codes is the first structure to be harmonised: whatever is said or done, it never carries the value given it by the *sender of the message* – it carries the value that *the receiver* attributes to it.

The important thing is not what is said: it is what is heard. Not what one is trying to express, but what is understood. We have to maintain our own un-renounceable ethical posture, and try to experience that of our interlocutors, the better to understand them.

Language separates as it brings closer

We have to be aware of our words and gestures, even of our dress, because each social group has different structures of meanings, and will understand the same symbols – verbal and gestural language, but also our physiognomy, our voice, the way we carry ourselves – only after translating them into their own personal idiom. As if, for each word or image, there were four dictionaries which defined it in four different tongues: four Codes.

The word spoken will never be the word heard: passing through the gates of the prison or the reformatory, we are entering a Semantic Tower of Babel. We have to be polyglot.

The theatre, sum of all languages, helps make dialogue possible. If I do not understand the word, I understand the gesture; if not the gesture, the sound; if not the sound, the silence; if not the silence, the tone; if not the tone, the movement. If I understand none of that, I understand the whole, which is greater than the sum of its parts. Our communication is rational, aesthetic and sensory; conscious and unconscious. The mind also speaks through the senses.

We have to separate the *deed* that was done from its *cause*; the *phenomenon*, which is always unique, *from the general law* which directs it. It is not our job to judge the crime; our job is to discover the causes so that the effects will not be repeated. We have to help everyone become conscious of the *meaning* of their acts.

Guards, prisoners, and we ourselves have to understand that, when we do Theatre of the Oppressed, we are not speaking of individual cases, of this or that particular prisoner or guard. We are studying moral behaviour and seeking ethical alternatives.

We have to create an effect of *shock* and *surprise* – without an explicit condemnation. When we show what happened, on stage, we have to investigate how it could have happened in another way. Every act is a choice! Fate does not exist. We construct our destiny. The future is invented.

TO has a *subjunctive* character: how might it have been? It is Socratic – asking questions. We have to work in such a way that each prisoner may discover truths for himself, with our help.

A peasant from Sergipe[10] said: 'The Theatre of the Oppressed is fantastic because, in it, you learn what you already knew!' Let me explain: we bring to consciousness the obscure, by seeing at a distance, in the *aesthetic space* of the stage, things that happen in real life right next to us, but without our registering them. Aesthetic distance allows a more all-embracing vision.

In São Paulo, a team of guards created a play in which the prisoners were played by the guards themselves. At the moment at which one of them, playing a prisoner, received the order to drop his head, raise his arms and spread his legs for inspection, for the first time he felt the humiliation he was used to inflicting, without being aware of it. *He saw the situation and saw himself in that situation* – that is theatre: seeing oneself seeing, observing oneself doing.

Another guard told us: 'Till yesterday I used to torture prisoners: now I have understood that what I used to do wasn't education like I thought it was – it was torture – which I know now: I don't want to be a torturer!'

A third told us that he had learnt nothing about Human Rights, the theme of our work – in spite of having participated for the whole year in everything that we had done. 'Nothing at all?' we asked. 'OK, I have learnt only that these prisoners aren't animals, like I used to think – they are human beings like us!' He had understood everything – aesthetically.

This is a Method to help people to think with their own minds, feel with their own emotions. We shall never be imperative, never give orders, or seek to convey the opinions of the sponsors of a programme.

Why Theatre of the Oppressed – why art?

Only with the birth of the human being, with the capacity to dream the future, are Culture, Art, Science and Invention born. Every human being is a producer of Culture, because Culture embraces all transformatory action carried out by human beings: not what they do, but the way they do it. Only the Human Being is capable of creating Culture.

The sentence of the prisoner is predicated on a limitation of his freedom in space, but it does not limit the activities of his mind, in time. Inactivity would be partial death, social death, the isolation of the human being in himself. No-one can be sentenced to immobilisation, to lobotomy of the imagination.

Justice does not deny the prisoner the right to grow intellectually. If he is to make right his wrongs, this growth is necessary. This is where Culture comes in. The human being is a creator, and each time that s/he creates something, other creations become necessary. Every discovery brings with it the necessity of new discoveries; every invention begs inventions.

When she creates Culture and invents Art, the human being achieves the feat of becoming human, without losing her animal condition. We cannot go back in time: I refuse to dwell in caves and I detest raw meat.

If I grasp hold of words that are in the dictionary, or words that run from mouth to mouth, if I order them as only I can, if I manipulate them, lengthen them, shorten them, change their sense; if I transform words, meanings, I invent syntaxes, rhymes, rhythms, and I write a poem, I will be transforming the reality of the words, and the act of transforming them transforms me into a poet – one who transforms words.

The same happens with theatre, when the spectator transforms herself into *spect-actor*, invades the stage and creates ideal images of what she wants to happen to her reality. The spectator transforms images of the society s/he sees and does not like, into images s/he sees and likes, images of a convivial society.

The act of transforming reality, even in image, is a transformative act, since *the image of the real is real as an image*! Theatre being the sum of all the arts, the spectator, invading the stage, transforms himself into sculptor, musician, poet; by going on stage, by showing his will, in action, by being the protagonist, the spectator transforms himself into the citizen! The prisoner transforms into the free man!

* * *

A PRIMER, NOT A CATECHISM

Useful suggestions

A recent festival, which featured groups performing from ten in the morning till seven in the evening, made me reflect on some important aspects of our work.

It was rewarding to see new Forum Theatre shows directed by *Multipliers* who had worked on the pieces for only twelve sessions, with casts made up of actors who had never set foot on a stage – these were people from communities, interested in discussing their problems, using theatre as the language.

It was fantastic to see the *capoeirista* who opened the Festival playing the National Anthem on her flute – including the whole of the second part, which almost no-one can remember. Equally fantastic was the fashion parade, elegantly executed by women my age and upwards – with weight and mass disposed to much greater advantage than mine! – showing dresses, shawls and other piece of clothing sewn by themselves, out of recycled cloth, not following the chic TV fashion shows, but only their own inclination and needs.

It was fantastic to see the artists from the neighbourhood showing their craft, in fabric, straw and ceramics.

On the flip side, the festival showed that we have to clarify certain aspects of our work to make things easier for those who use our Method.

Barbarity and Civilisation: *Civilisation*, if I remember rightly, is characterised by the existence, in a given society, of values and customs codified into laws and commandments accepted as just or necessary, and which can be obeyed or transgressed, but not ignored. It is characterised by the existence of projects common to the society which produces these values, or is forced to accept them.

These values do not necessarily have to be of a humanistic and altruistic nature: it is enough for them to exist. The civilisation does not need to attain a particular degree of sophistication: it is enough that it has such values, for it to attain the title of 'civilisation'.

When people talk about *primitive societies*, in reality, they are speaking of societies whose complexities, being different from ours, we are unable to perceive, just as the members of those societies do not perceive our complexities.

The Greeks and Romans called foreigners *barbarians*. The *barbarian* was the person who did not speak our language – they spoke their own – did not have our customs – they had their own – would not obey our laws, and did obey their own. Consequently, they were appropriated to become our slaves

– not being the same as us, we considered them to be inferior. If they were like us, they could not be our slaves; if they were like us, that would mean they were morally permitted to enslave us one day.

Today, the term *barbarity* no longer designates societies with values that are different from ours, but those in which values do not exist, or laws, or rules, or common projects – only individual or group projects – societies in which each citizen makes their own ethics.

In Brazil, we have been victims of successive dictatorships – explicit dictatorship, in the time of the military, and implicit, from then on – which habituated the people not to believe in anything and to hold everything in contempt, except the quick buck. Courage, as a value, has been replaced by cunning; fidelity, by opportunism; honour, by appearances.

Our notion of respect towards others is less than rigid. In our daily lives, we are not civilised: we are *barbarians*.

As a consequence, the people, not used to being respected, are unfamiliar with the notion of respect: it is not a question of bad faith, they are simply not conscious of the effects of what they do, of the transgressions they perpetrate. For instance: crossing the road outside the designated crossing points; bribing traffic police or tax inspectors to avoid fines; singing at full volume in the early hours beneath the windows of innocent sleepers; moving chairs around during an emotional scene in the theatre.

We must not fall into the trap of allowing the *normal* conditions of the locale where we are going to work to continue to be *normal*, when an event that is absolutely *abnormal* – the theatre show! – is happening in this space.

In the street, it is impossible to stop the drunkard declaiming his ills to the world; or children running and shouting; or passers-by passing, chatting away to each other; or cars honking their horns or motorcyclists scaring the living daylights out of us on their pizza delivery runs. In the street, that's just the way it is.

The street has its Aesthetic, just as the stage of the *Comédie Française* has its Aesthetic. Shakespeare started his plays using the device of making more noise on stage than the noise of some spectators in the audience: *Romeo and Juliet* starts with a ferocious knife fight between opposing factions; *Hamlet* with a cadaverous phantasm risen from Purgatory – where he is stuck awaiting better nights – demanding vengeance from his son, asking him to kill the king, the young man's uncle; *Macbeth* has barely begun when up jump witches ugly as the plague, come from the Devil knows where, prophesying bloody futures; in *Richard III*, the eponymous deformed monster, whose own shadow makes him jump, swears to marry the beautiful widow of the man who he has just murdered and whose funeral cortege is at that moment approaching . . . And so on.

In the well-behaved *Comédie* of today, when Molière's classic works are played, the light drops, the curtain rises, and the audience, as professional as the actors, confine themselves to silence.

As for us, even when we work in closed spaces, we are neither Shakespeare nor *Comédie*. Before we begin a show, we must eliminate all sources of distraction, in terms of sight or sound, that could take us away from it. The show should never just be started, any old how, in the middle of a great clamour, just because it is getting late. *Forum should be joyful but it shouldn't turn into a free-for-all.*

The Rectangle: when we find ourselves in a rectangular space, which is frequently, we should set up our stage in the middle of one of the longer sides of this rectangle, with the audience all round the three other sides, like a flattened horseshoe, with their backs to the light coming through doors and windows. If the stage is placed on one of the smaller sides, we end up with more rows of seating in front of the stage and stretching back from it. By doing as I have described, there will be less than half the rows of seats, and the audience are closer to the actors, facilitating their interventions. The closer they are to the stage, the more courageous the *spect-actors* are.

When putting up the set, the question should never be 'Where is the audience going to go?', but rather 'Where are they not going to go?' And they should not be on only one of four sides.

Our *Aesthetic Space* should be like the Roman amphitheatre rather than the Italian stage, invented by a theatre designer called Serlio,[11] almost at the end of the Renaissance, when the idea was to give the show the appearance of a living picture, since Renaissance painters had just invented the third dimension, perspective, which was almost absent from medieval painting, thereby creating the illusion of reality. The *Serlian* stage was distant and untouchable; ours is penetrable. He aimed at separating the new aristocrats (the bourgeois, the characters) from the people (the audience).

Oppressed and Oppressors: the *Oppressed* is not defined in relation to him- or herself (except when using the *Introspective Techniques of the Rainbow of Desires*) but in relation to the *Oppressor*. The Oppressed is the person who asks the question: what would you do in my place? He or she is the person who is to be replaced in order to seek out and rehearse alternatives to the oppressive situation presented in the *model* – the scene or play which serves as introduction to the Forum.

I think it is bad if the audience is asked: 'Do you identify with any oppressed person in this scene?'

This approach gives the impression that we do not know what we are asking. When the scene itself is already the formulation of a question, it becomes clear that the formulator of the question is the Oppressed themselves, and this should become evident in the body of the show. The

Oppressed is he or she who attempts to achieve some kind of act of liberation and fails.

Forum Theatre is a question sincerely asked of the audience, in the form of a theatrical scene. It is the sincere desire to confront diverse opinions, ideas, actions. The Oppressed is the one asking the question – and the question must be asked clearly.

Of course, the Forum must be done on the scene chosen by the public, because that's what they want – however it must always be made clear that, when the question changes, the forum will be responding to this new question and not to the original one; consequently, the subject under debate will be changed. After this forum, we must go on to the scene we have originally suggested.

When writing or analysing the structure of a play meant to be done in Forum, it is fundamental to start at the Nucleus of Conflict, Protagonist versus Antagonists – this should be the concretion of the Central Idea or Theme, which is inevitably abstract and general, like *racism, sexism, imperialism*, etc. The Idea is the Brain, the Nucleus of Conflict, the Heart. All other elements derive from this. No theatre scene can stand on its feet without Brain and Heart. When I say this, I am not being romantic, but precise.

The Aestheticisation of the Image: this is one of the most important aspects of our work, with which we have to take the greatest care. The *image* is also an actor in the presentation, though its effect may be on an unconscious level. The audience may not register what they see, but they see it, even if this vision does not pass through their alert consciousness.

If we put a table and two chairs on stage, the chairs and the table will be speaking all the time and saying, non-stop, things that chairs and tables say. If, in two plays following on from each other – with different characters, stories and subject matter – the same chairs and the same table stay on stage, during the second piece they will continue saying, monotonously, the same things they were saying in the first, even though that piece was about other subjects and with other characters.

I have heard Jokers saying: 'I so wanted to put such and such a thing on the stage, but we don't have time, let's go without it . . .' In fact, in such cases, not only do you go ahead *lacking* the object which was so necessary, but, which is worse, you go ahead with an empty space taking the place of this object.

'I wanted to put a quilt on top of the bed, a brightly coloured quilt, patterned with blue flowers, but I went ahead anyhow . . .' In its place stands the wooden truckle bed: not only does the flowered quilt not speak its lines, but, in its place, the wooden truckle bed never shuts its mouth, and the audience is left receiving messages from the dark wood and not from the coloured cloth; from the colour of death, rather than from living colours.

In the place of one thing, another thing is always left, *even if it is only the absence of the first thing*. Image is Language as important as the Word. These two languages need to speak to each other, harmoniously, because from this dialogue will emerge something that neither one, on its own, would be able to say.

Never say: 'It'll do as it is . . .' – because it won't; it will be doing something else. Instead of what you wanted it to say, it will be saying something different.

Never should an object be used on stage, whatever it may be, in exactly the way it is found within the home or in the shop window. All Images must be *aestheticised*, modified, transformed, in such a way that they will contain the opinion of the group about the object, be it a table, a chair, a hat, a tie, a door, an earring, a cow, a horse, a goat, a feather-duster, anything whatsoever that is seen: image.

Image is Ideological: if we need a telephone, the only thing we must not put on stage is a real telephone. If we do use one, we must we change its colour, its size, or cut it up leaving the wires showing, or place ten phones on top of each other, sprayed yellow or violet – these are just ideas off the top of my head. The point is that the telephone cannot come straight out of the shop and on to the stage, because it will come invested with the ideology of the shop.

If we *aestheticise* the phone, it will translate our opinion; unless we do that, it will speak the opinion of its manufacturer. Every object should always be the carrier of an opinion, of a value, a significance, an ideology.

Hot Objects: apart from the space within it, the Image must be filled entirely with objects which have a meaning, a significance: *Hot Objects*. We should not create *décor* (as the French call it), simply furnishing a space by filling the spaces in it – rather we should seek to place on stage objects that are 'ideologically characterised'. In the same way that a character only exists if he or she has a significance for the drama, and if she or he exerts a *Will* inside a system of conflicting *Wills*, so an object must only go on stage if its absence would be a loss. The forum develops not only through the words spoken on the stage, but also through the objects on it.

The Pre-Theory of the Unusual Object: one day when I was in the North-East, I went into a little church, and was stopped in my tracks by the sight of a donkey staring at the image of Christ on the cross, in the middle of the evening mass. The donkey understood nothing of religion, obviously, but I understood a lot of things seeing the donkey gazing at the altar: I understood that this was an *unusual combination*.

The donkey was in a place where it absolutely could not be, and that for me *en-stranged*[12] not only the animal, but everything around it: the statues, the flowers and the saints. It made me look with fresh eyes at the faithful congregants kneeling in prayer, unaware of the impertinent asinine presence, composed in their role of worshippers, an image which was discomposed by this jument-ine invasion.

The presence of the *Unusual Object* in a scenario with which we would never associate it – in this case, the *Unusual Object* was the inquisitive donkey and the scenario, the little church – made me *see* what, without it, I would merely have looked at; the faithful, the priest and rosary, all normal, as normal as a donkey grazing in a field. What was not normal was the presence of the donkey in the church, lost in thought – it caused shock, surprise and wonder.

The donkey, feeling uncomfortable, left straight after the homily, without being noticed by the priest who, alas, was myopic and deaf, and saw nothing to trouble him, outside his liturgical affairs.

Any unaccustomed presence attracts curiosity, not only about itself, but about *everything around it*.

In my campaign for *Vereador*-ship[13] in 1992, we performed what was more or less an *Invisible Theatre* scene, whose setting was a classroom, complete with exercise books, blackboard, nuns and pupils, performed on Ipanema beach. It was a protest against an obscene increase in the monthly fees of a religious school.

On the sands of Copacabana, men and women, dressed in black and singing funereal hymns, dug graves and threw flowers into the open holes, in protest against the dangers of the Angra 3 nuclear power station[14] – a plant about which there were many safety concerns. Between one hymn and the next, the actors explained to the assembled bathers the likelihood of an accidental explosion – in which eventuality they would need thousands of graves like those they were digging.

In both cases, theatricality was used to emphasise the subject matter – and it was produced by this unusual superposition of scenarios: the church and its incompatible donkey; the classroom and the cemetery on the sun-drenched beaches.

Of course, you do not need to search far and wide for donkeys or nun's habits. According to the *Theory of the Unusual Object*, when the Joker doesn't have at her disposition any other means of aestheticising her image, she can cast around for any discrepant object, any object which collides or clashes with the normal scenario, causing a *fissure* in our perception of the Image.

It can be a pile of rags thrown on the ground, like a carpet; a yellow cloth draped at the back of the set, like a flag; a white cloth covering the rocking chair, like a shroud, or a mannequin on the sofa, as if dead.

This can be done when no object with ideological connotations can be found; the *surprise* effect is obtained, which will help us look carefully, with an analytical eye.

This is a pre-theory: we are going to develop it.

Recorded Music and Invented Instruments: recorded music does not go with the Theatre of the Oppressed, nor with any other form of theatre. It delivers us up to technology and brings to mind recording studios, industrial production. Live sound is alive. We must invent new instruments, without abandoning the guitar, the *reco-reco*[15] and the *cavaquinho*.[16]

Dramaturgy: when the script is written, the result is better, the actors more secure and better prepared for the Forum. The thing to be improvised is the *Forum*, not the *model*, which must recount all the elements essential for the *Oppressed's Question* to be clear and to allow creative interventions.

When you read the written script, you can see what is lacking, and what is superfluous. The written word is visible and reveals its meanings and potentialities.

Dramaturgy is based on a Structure of Conflicts. We must always remember the four essential elements of a theatre scene:

1 *The conflict*: the collision, the clash of the *Conscious Wills to achieve their goals* and of the means they employ; those means should be *Objective and Subjective*, concrete and abstract, concrete facts which have ideological significations. The character WANTS before BEING. Do not come on stage without knowing what you want to do there. Before coming on, always say: 'I want . . .' and complete the phrase. Of course, these wills must be socially *necessary*, not casual or whimsical; we could say that the scene is a Structure of Necessary wills.

2 *Quantitative Movement:* this is the *Dramatic Action* (the development of the drama, of the structure of necessary conflictual wills), including the *Counter-Preparation*, which entails beginning the scene a good distance before the *Chinese Crisis*[17] (which is the moment in which the protagonist has to take a definitive and irreversible decision); in the Forum theatre model, the decision will lead to disaster, which will enable the spectators, by intervening, to find alternatives.

3 *Qualitative Movement, Chinese Crisis*: when the structure of the conflict changes in quality – which is, usually, the moment at which the spect-actors are going to intervene. The decision has been taken! The same model can have more than one *Chinese Crisis* and the spect-actors can intervene before any of them happen if they consider that it will be too late if they leave it till then.

4 *Unity of Theatrical Elements*: all the elements of the show must be

structured according to the theme of the play, and must always be in concordance with it: Image, Sound, Characters, Side Conflicts, etc.

Forms of Identification: this is another frequent query: who can take the place of whom? In fact, for a spect-actor to come on stage, there has to be a strong relationship of identity between him or her and the Protagonist. This can be on three levels:

1 absolute *identity*, when the Protagonist incarnates exactly the same problem as the audience faces;
2 *analogy*, when the audience's problem is not exactly what is shown, but strong analogies exist between the two;
3 *solidarity*: the audience's concerns are not identical, nor analogical, but a relationship of deep solidarity allows the spect-actor to offer his or her sensibility and knowledge to try to open up a range of possibilities, so that the Protagonist may find solutions to his own problem.

The Will to Fight: the Oppressed Protagonist cannot be a Lazarus, because the Theatre of the Oppressed is not Jesus Christ and cannot bring anyone back from the dead. The Protagonist must be someone who is fighting, though without knowledge of the possibilities open to her, possibilities which will be examined in the Forum. The audience must feel that the Protagonist is fighting so that they will identify themselves with her, and want to help her with their interventions, thereby helping themselves by practising this exercise of liberty.

The Che Guevara Syndrome: we must steer clear of the thought that all situations, however desperate, have solutions. Che believed, romantically, that it would be enough to create a focus of rebellion against the Bolivian dictatorship for the peasants to rebel and create hundreds of other foci, as had been done in Cuba; in Cuba, however, the people were already in a state of revolt and ready for the struggle when the spark was lit. When we are doing a Forum, we have to be honest and cautious: romantic, but realistic. We have to analyse the possibilities, but avoid the illusion of magic solutions!

When You Don't Know What to Say, Ask!: The Forum is a *Space of Liberty* and the Joker is the person who must assure the exercise of this liberty. She has the function of organising the theatrical debate, clarifying – by means of questions and the exposition of her own perception, which should not be hidden – the meaning of each intervention.

You should not waste time with long explanations before the beginning of the show, nor should you, after each intervention, allow the room to transform itself into a public meeting; the more theatre, the better; the more that theatrical language is used, rather than only verbal language, the more we will learn, aesthetically. It is important, however, that each intervention is not reduced to a physical act; we must clarify the importance of this act and its significance. We must verbalise the act.

When the Joker does not know how to respond, she should, sincerely, ask the audience what do to. If you don't know, for sure somebody in the audience does.

The Couch Potato and the Brick Wall: the former is the actor playing the part of an oppressor, who does not react to new elements introduced by spect-actors; he just observes what they do and stops there, without carrying on the improvisation – when it is precisely this continuation of the improvisation which is going to help us understand the possibilities and nature of each intervention. This is the *Couch Potato*. The *Brick Wall*, by contrast, massacres the spect-actor, saying always no, no, no, by means of continual negatives blocking the continuation of the debate. *Couch Potatoes* and *Brick Walls* confuse and hinder the operation of the Forum.

The Rhythm of the Forum: just as much as in a normal show, the Forum, which is theatre and must have theatricality, needs the right rhythm. I am not talking about speed, but rhythm, which is the pleasing organisation of time. Both model and Forum are theatre!

Characterisation and Motivation: it is not enough for the characters to do – this *doing* needs to be coloured. Motivation is what the characters want and are pursuing; characterisation is their individualised way of pursuing and doing what they want. The characterisation must be attended to with care, since frequently that is where the oppression resides: in the way of doing, rather than in what is done.

Yes, But . . .: one of the rehearsal techniques which can be useful in the creation of the characters is called 'Yes, but . . .': each actor always has to agree with what the other says and then set out a contradiction, a doubt, an impossibility. The interlocutor will respond in the same format: 'You are right, yes, but . . .'

Sagas: many groups have the tendency to tell their life stories, in interminable sagas: theatre is the art of crises, it deals with critical, decisive moments. Clearly we must include the dramatic elements which the group considers essential; however, from the theatrical point of view, the whole life of each individual – so essential in the reality of each individual – on stage can be too much to take. *Theatre is the Art of Synthesis*.

The Aesthetic Education of the Oppressed: this we cannot forget. We have to try and stimulate not only the theatrical aspects, but all the aesthetic facets of every participant – and each time more than the last.

Remember, it is not the finished product which is of greatest interest; it is the act of writing, painting, sculpting, singing, composing, dancing. It is the care with which the words, colours, movements, are chosen and the desire to learn new ones; the more we know, the better prepared we will be to think thoughts which only these words, movements, colours, can express and make us feel.

To make a sculpture is even easier than to write a poem, for instance, because poets have to deal with what they are not seeing and cannot touch – words – while sculptors deal with visible and sensible matter. Here's what we call *Human Being Out of Rubbish*: we ask the participants in each group to collect 'clean rubbish' from their community or from the milieu of their work. With these objects, we ask them to make a human figure – at work, at play, in love, etc. And they do it. They have total freedom to add colour, paints etc.

I believe that to make music is even easier: isn't it what children do when they kick things they find on their way – drawing music from these objects?

It is simple, very simple, but it is not so simple: this is the beginning. The Spanish poet Antonio Machado says: '*Caminante, no hay camino: se hace camino al andar*' ('Wayfarer, there is no way; the way is made by walking').

Andemos – let's walk.

Notes

1 The Titan (Prometheus) did what he thought right: he gave man fire, till then the private property of the gods. He democratised fire. The gods, however, were not prepared for democracy. They wanted to keep fire for themselves alone. They feared that – feeling the lure of fire – men would also want to own the earth that bore them, the water that quenched their thirst, and the fruit that killed their hunger, which would be too much. It would be happiness.

2 Command – the drug-traffickers use the same terminology as the army to designate their groupings. AJ

3 When a guard administers corporal punishment to young people, which happens often, he is violating the same Penal Code the young people themselves violated. He is violating both the Universal Declaration of Human Rights and the Constitution of the country, which do not permit corporal punishment, or other cruel or degrading punishments: people who degrade themselves in this way – by degrading, by committing physical and moral offence to those they should be protecting – what authority can they possibly have to exercise their authority?

4 A big land-owner, proprietor of *latifúndia*. AJ

5 Some of our Jokers immediately recognised some of the young people in the reformatories as old neighbours or childhood friends of theirs.

6 A young man, asked about what theme he would like the play we were about to create to have, answered: 'How to kill a Judge'. When met with our refusal, he continued: 'Who can I kill, then?'

7 Or educators, or guards. Here, I use the generic term 'agents', in the full knowledge that in various prisons the function of educator, or social worker, is more important.

8 In the recent past, asylums were accursed places where the deranged perambulated round the buildings, without direction, naked and hungry. They awaited death as today the prisoners await the end of their punishment or death in fratricidal struggles within the prisons.

9 I cannot hide that I was prisoner and have felt what they feel; I know the importance of time and space in the life of a prisoner and can remember what it felt like; but I have never been a guard or other prison official – I can only imagine.

10 A state in the North-East of Brazil. AJ

11 Italian architect and stage designer Sebastiano Serlio (1475–1554). AJ

12 The Portuguese word used is: *estranhar* – to make strange. AJ

13 *Vereador* – legislator, in the Rio de Janeiro chamber. For an account of this campaign for election in Rio de Janeiro, see *The Legislative Theatre*, Augusto Boal, Routledge 1998. AJ

14 An unfinished nuclear power station, outside Rio de Janeiro, which had been mothballed for fifteen years when discussions about completing it were revived in 2001. AJ

15 *Reco-reco*: Brazilian percussion instrument of Angolan origin, consisting of a length of bamboo with transverse notches cut into it, over which a wand is rubbed to produce a rasping intermittent sound. AJ

16 *Cavaquinho*: a musical instrument resembling a small guitar, with four steel strings, generating a high-pitched and loud sound – an important instrument in Samba and Choro. AJ

17 In Chinese, there is apparently no single ideogram for the word 'crisis': there are two, which mean 'danger' and 'opportunity'. AJ

SEVENTIETH BIRTHDAY – 2001

THE BIRTHDAY SPEECH

When I turned seventy, on the 16 March 2001, my friends held a party for me at the *Teatro Nelson Rodrigues*, where we were doing a TO festival, and they asked me to say something. This is what I said, in so many words:

I agreed to this event on two conditions: the first, that all our closest friends be invited, and so they were – only the closest: the 500 odd of you here, and several hundred others who could not come – only our dearest friends. Welcome.

The second condition was that you would have to swear not to tell anyone that I am seventy years old, because when I was young my image of a septuagenarian was of a little old man seated on a seaside bench, watching the waves fading in the sand, cigar dangling from the corner of his mouth, walking stick in his right hand and dog at his left foot. I swear that I have neither dog nor stick.

I also had two reasons to accept the homage, one *bona fide*, and the other . . . well, you can tell me.

The *bona fide* reason is the centre of the Theatre of the Oppressed, this ship sailed by those magnificent people Bárbara, Claudete, Helen, Geo and Olivar – the five current jokers, many others having passed through, some thousands having travelled part of the journey with us – I have always thought that this centre deserves visibility for the work it does. An event like this informs and reveals. That's the *bona fide* reason.

The more dubious reason is that I am jealous. And the great culprit is the poet Ferreira Gullar, a dear friend here present. Why?

Months ago, invited to Gullar's seventieth birthday party, I went, happy for my friend and fearful, imagining that at seventy he would already be stooped over and feeble-voiced. When I arrived at the party, I saw an exuberant and handsome Gullar, brimming with health and happiness, talking about the future, his plans, the play that he had just finished writing and that he had the courage to invite me to direct. Gullar pulverised the image that I had of the seventy-year old man.

Being given to envy, I thought to myself: 'When I grow up, I am going to be seventy years old like Gullar and you won't find me putting a saucer down for the cat and feeding the pigeons!'

I was left turning over these envious thoughts, waiting for the day when I would equal Gullar, at least in age, the day of my seventieth, but I wasn't expecting this day to arrive so soon. It turned out to be the most rapidly satisfied wish I have ever had.

Days ago, I heard it said that Oscar Niemeyer discovered, at ninety-three, that he still did not know how to play the guitar. So he contracted a teacher, and in the following mornings woke his neighbours with celestial chords.

My strong envy attacked afresh; I took myself to task and, grinding my teeth, I said to myself: – 'Grrrr . . . One day, I am going to be like Oscar Niemeyer. I am going to learn to sing in tune, because to date, the only instrument that I have learnt to play, more or less well, is the trumpet – when it comes to trumpeting the wrongs of the world, I can hold my own.

I promised myself – and for sure, one day, I am going to learn to play the sitar like Ravi Shankar, the cello like Pablo Casals, the violin like Yehudi Menuhin, and, while I am at it, I am going to do death-defying leaps like Madonna, without dropping a note, one octave above middle C. I assure you, it will have been worth the wait.

I have already chosen the first piece of my repertoire: *Samba on a Single Note*. I am starting by learning this note and then, with more leisure and if there is time over, I will learn two or three more. For me, it's enough to be going on with.

Why do I want to keep my age secret, if I already have Gullar and Niemeyer as sources of envy and example? Because I believe that, if you don't manage to forget that I am seventy, I am going to end up being seventy!

I believe that people end up being the age that others think they are. It starts with the way people look at one – only after this does one take on an old person's face, manner, body, and gait. For which reason, please don't look at me in that way; rather think of me on my fortieth, which was just the other day.

To illustrate this well-grounded fear, this dependency on the opinion of others, I am going to tell a story that an English director told me last year: he was staging *King Lear* and he invited an excellent actor to play the part of the King.

During the rehearsals, Richard, the actor in question, moved even his colleagues – who are, as is well-known, the most savage audience there is. In the scene in which he divides his kingdom between his daughters, Richard was superb. With thunderous and voluptuous voice, he bellowed:

'Goneril, do you love me?'

'My father, I love you more than I love the sea and the mountains, the earth and the stars!'

'Great. So should a daughter love her father, especially in my house. You are going to get a third of my Kingdom! And you, Regan?', he thundered deafeningly.

'I love you more than my life!'

'Wonderful! You are going to take the second third of my kingdom. And you, Cordelia, last but not least, I want you to say something more than your sisters, to avoid an anticlimax.'[1]

'Nothing' – answered Cordelia and the cast trembled before this genius actor and his dinosaur-sized anger.

'Nothing will come of nothing; speak again!'

'My father, I love you as a daughter should love her father, and when I get married I will also love my husband, do you understand me?'

Even the seats in the auditorium were terrified and wanted to flee. They shook in their fixings. They lifted the nails which anchored them and fled through the doors at a run, while the king cursed Cordelia with a voice like thunder and lightning on a stormy night peopled with Ariels and Calibans plus witches from Macbeth.

My director friend was so happy that he resolved to invite some of his least-loved colleagues and friends to the dress rehearsal to arouse their envy and jealousy. Before they went on, the director went to warn his cast of the presence of this illustrious audience He thanked them all, especially Richard for his stupendous performance. Richard modestly replied:

'Not a word of it . . . you deserve the credit, as the excellent director you are . . . you taught me almost everything I know. But the character still isn't there yet, I still need to add the finishing touches – who knows, maybe you can help me one more time . . . For instance, I do not know the King's age . . .'

The director answered that he thought that Lear could be seventy odd, and Richard seemed dazzled by the discovery:

'See what I mean? That is going to help me complete the character, because age is very important. You are a top director! Today, Lear will come out better than ever. Seventy years old! What a fine age. *The yellow leaf*! Marvellous!'

The rehearsal started, as wonderful as ever, till Lear came on, leaning on a stick: a turn-up for the books! The director shuddered, thinking that perhaps Richard had twisted his ankle going down a step, like Orson Welles who took a tumble on the day of his opening of the same play and performed the part ensconced in a wheelchair.

Richard declaimed his text, with a hoarse and feeble voice:

'Goneril . . ., do you . . . like . . . me?'

'Ah, dear father, don't do this to me: I love you more than I love the rivers and the mountains, the sky and the sea . . .,' said the daughter, flabbergasted at the voice and the stick.

'Take a third . . . of my kingdom . . . and off you go. You Regan, now it is your turn; speak loudly, because I am going deaf . . . the ebb of life . . .'

'Dear father, for the love of God, stop this: I love you more than I love life itself,' wailed Regan, stunned.

'Take another third. And you, baby girl, it is your turn, grasp the opportunity, Cordelia.'

'Nothing.'

Lear shook with anger, virtually going into a death-rattle, an epileptic fit on the floor, his strangled voice murdering the Shakespearian verse.

The director stood up, spitting with fury, ordered the curtain to be dropped and exploded:

'Have you gone mad? You are destroying my show!'

'I am giving it the final gloss. Lear is seventy – that is fundamental to his psychological and physical characterisation. An old man, seventy years old goes around bent over and speaks almost voicelessly, . . . like this . . . eeeehhhh . . .' answered the actor, with the feeble voice of the character which was now, according to him, fully achieved.

Defeated, the director still had the strength to ask:

'So what about you, Richard, how old are you?'

'Me? I have just turned seventy – seventy years of a life lived to the full!' he retorted jubilantly, loud and clear, forgetting his age, his supposed *old* age.

To finish, I want to say that there is a third reason why I accepted this honour: in 2001, there are many round-numbered anniversaries that we are commemorating. Ten years of my working with the current CTO-Rio team; fifteen years since the establishment of Centre of the Theatre of the Oppressed of Rio de Janeiro; twenty years since Cecilia and I started our research into *The Rainbow of Desire*, when we were still in exile in France; thirty since the start of the Theatre of the Oppressed, which was born in São Paulo; forty-five since my debut as director of the Arena Theatre; seventy years of my short life – tell no-one – and, *last but not least*, 35 years since Cecilia and I decided to get married.

Cecilia, this anniversary is also yours – and this party is yours.

Note

1 This was clearly a loose version of Shakespeare's text.

Related titles from Routledge

A Boal Companion:
Dialogues on Theatre and Cultural Politics
edited by Jan Cohen-Cruz and Mady Schutzman

This carefully constructed and thorough collection of theoretical engagements with Augusto Boal's work is the first to look 'beyond Boal' and critically assesses the Theatre of the Oppressed (TO) movement in context.

A Boal Companion looks at the cultural practices which inform TO and explore them within a larger frame of cultural politics and performance theory. The contributors put TO into dialogue with complexity theory – Merleau-Ponty, Emmanuel Levinas, race theory, feminist performance art, Deleuze and Guattari, and liberation psychology – to name just a few, and in doing so, the kinship between Boal's project and multiple fields of social psychology, ethics, biology, comedy, trauma studies and political science is made visible.

The ideas generated throughout *A Boal Companion* will:

- expand readers' understanding of TO as a complex, interdisciplinary, multivocal body of philosophical discourses
- provide a variety of lenses through which to practise and critique TO
- make explicit the relationship between TO and other bodies of work.

This collection is ideal for TO practitioners and scholars who want to expand their knowledge, but it also provides unfamiliar readers and new students to the discipline with an excellent study resource.

ISBN10: 0–415–32293–6 (hbk)
ISBN10: 0–415–32294–4 (pbk)

ISBN13: 978–0–415–32293–5 (hbk)
ISBN13: 978–0–415–32294–2 (pbk)

Available at all good bookshops
For ordering and further information please visit:
www.routledge.com

Related titles from Routledge

**Games for Actors and Non-Actors 2nd Edition
by Augusto Boal**

'Boal's analysis of the art of the Actor makes *Games for Actors and Non-Actors* compulsory reading.'

Plays and Players

'This is a useful handbook for those who want to explore Boal's Theatre of the Oppressed and as such is greatly to be welcomed. Boal's work deserves and demands emulation.'

Theatre Research International

Games for Actors and Non-Actors is the classic and best selling book by the founder of Theatre of the Oppressed, Augusto Boal. It sets out the principles and practice of Boal's revolutionary method, showing how theatre can be used to transform and liberate everyone – actors and non-actors alike!

This thoroughly updated and substantially revised second edition includes:

- two new essays by Boal on major recent projects in Brazil;
- Boal's description of his work with the Royal Shakespeare Company;
- a revised introduction and translator's preface;
- a collection of photographs taken during Boal's workshops, commissioned for this edition;
- new reflections on Forum Theatre.

ISBN10: 0–415–26761–7 (hbk)
ISBN10: 0–415–26708–0 (pbk)

ISBN13: 978–0–415–26761–8 (hbk)
ISBN13: 978–0–415–26708–3 (pbk)

Available at all good bookshops
For ordering and further information please visit:
www.routledge.com

Related titles from Routledge

**Hamlet and the Baker's Son:
My Life in Theatre and Politics
by Augusto Boal**

Hamlet and the Baker's Son is the autobiography of Augusto Boal, inventor of the internationally renowned Forum Theatre system, the 'Theatre of the Oppressed' and author of *Games for Actors and Non-Actors* and *Legislative Theatre*. Continuing to travel the world giving workshops and inspiration to teachers, prisoners, actors and care-workers, Augusto Boal is a visionary as well as a product of his times – the Brazil of military dictatorship and artistic and social repression – and was once imprisoned for his subversive activities.

From his early days in Brazil's political theatre movement to his recent experiments with theatre as a democratic political process, Boal's story is a moving and memorable one. He has devised a unique way of using the stage to empower the disempowered, and taken his methods everywhere from the favelas of Rio to the rehearsal studios of the Royal Shakespeare Company.

ISBN10: 0–415–22988–X (hbk)
ISBN10: 0–415–22989–8 (pbk)

ISBN13: 978–0–415–22988–3 (hbk)
ISBN13: 978–0–415–22989–0 (pbk)

Available at all good bookshops
For ordering and further information please visit:
www.routledge.com